AKBAR-NAMA
OF
SHAIKH ABU-L FAZL

AKBAR-NAMA
OF
SHAIKH ABU-L FAZL

EDITED BY: JOHN DOWSON

GYAN

Published by

GYAN

Gyan Publishing House
5, Ansari Road
Daryaganj, New Delhi-110002
Phone: 011-47034999, 9811692060
E-mail: books@gyanbooks.com

Distribution Network
gyanbooks.com
India, USA, Canada, UK, Australia

ISBN: 978-93-6433-006-0 (HB)
First Published, 1857

2nd Impression 2024

Printed at: Gyan Press, Delhi.

AKBAR-NAMA OF SHAIKH ABU-L FAZL
EDITOR: JOHN DOWSON

AKBAR-NÁMA

OF

SHAIKH ABÚ-L FAZL.

AKBAR-NÁMA

OF

SHAIKH ABÚ-L FAZL.

[ABÚ-L FAZL 'ALLÁMÍ was the son of Shaikh Mubárak, son of Shaikh Khizr, who emigrated from Sind to Hindústán. Shaikh Mubárak was born at Nágor, and at an early age gave evidence of great intellectual powers. He became one of the most learned men of the time, and was conspicuous during the reign of Akbar for his great erudition and his liberal opinions on religious matters. He had several sons, two of whom rose to the greatest eminence and celebrity. The eldest, Shaikh Abú-l Faiz, better known as Faizí, was the most popular poet of the time. He was a great favourite and the constant companion of Akbar, who gave him the title of "Prince of Poets." His compositions are still held in very high estimation, as second only to those of Amír Khusrú, the acknowledged chief of Indian poets.

Abú-l Fazl was the second son, and was born on the 14th January, 1551. He was educated under his father's care, and was a devoted student. His range of reading was extensive, and before the age of twenty he had obtained the reputation of being a deep and critical scholar. His attainments afterwards gained for him the high-sounding title of *'Allámí*.

Faizí's poems early attracted the attention of the Emperor, who invited the young poet to his Court while he was engaged in the siege of Chítor, in the twelfth year of the reign. Faizí soon became an established favourite, and enjoyed great influence. By his means Abú-l Fazl was introduced at Court in his seventeenth year. His abilities were immediately recognized, and every year he grew in favour and in power, until he rose to the office of Prime Minister, and became a *mansabdár* of 4000. In the position of courtier and minister he enjoyed the unbounded confidence of the Emperor, and he discharged his duties, both as a civilian and a soldier, with distinguished ability and success. In the following pages some passages will be found relating to his services in the Dakhin, and an incident connected with the siege of Ásír deserves to be here recorded to his honour. Bahádur Khán, the holder of this fortress, was desirous of gaining the favour of Abú-l Fazl, hoping by his influence to avert the Emperor's displeasure. He therefore sent him some rich presents. Abú-l Fazl returned the presents with the following statement: "I have made a vow not to accept presents till four conditions are fulfilled. 1. Friendship. 2. That I should not value the gift too highly. 3. That I should not have been anxious to get a present. 4. Necessity to accept it. Now, supposing that the first three are satisfied in the present case, the favour of the Emperor has extinguished every desire in me of accepting gifts from others."

Both Faizí and Abú-l Fazl imbibed the liberal opinions of their father, and carried them to greater extremes. They were reviled by the faithful as heterodox, as apostates, as heretics, as free-thinkers, as perverters of the truth and deceivers of the faithful. Akbar's tolerance, his early doubts, and his inquiries into the principles of other religions, had shown themselves before the brothers were introduced at Court. But if they did not kindle the fire, they fanned it and kept it alive. In them the Emperor found congenial minds, with feelings and opinions similar to but more decided than his own. With them he held frequent converse, and indulged his partiality for theological discussion. The result was that he and they, mutually influencing each other, progressed through various phases of scepticism and credulity, until they finally arrived at the rejection of Islám, and the establishment of the "Divine Faith," described as "Divine Monotheism." At the head of this new religion stood Akbar himself; next after him came Abú-l Fazl and Faizí.

Prince Salím, afterwards the Emperor Jahángír, had a great dislike of Abú-l Fazl. The minister served his master too faithfully, and thwarted the ambitious views of the heir so successfully, as to make himself an object of hatred. "He was no friend of mine," wrote Jahángír in his Memoirs, and he took an opportunity to remove the man he feared and hated. The Prince had more than once shown signs of rebellion, and of an intention to assume independence. In the forty-seventh year of his father's reign his ambitious designs displayed themselves more distinctly, and excited much distrust in the mind of the Emperor. At this time Abú-l Fazl was in command in the Dakhin, and Akbar, desiring the support and counsel of his trusty minister, sent him an urgent recall. Abú-l Fazl obeyed the summons immediately, and set out for Ágra with only a slender escort. This afforded the opportunity for making an end of him. A Bundela Rájá, named Bír Singh, was incited by the Prince to waylay the minister, and kill him. Abú-l Fazl had warning of his danger, but refused to turn aside. On Friday, the 4th Rabí'u-l awwal (12th August, 1602), he was attacked by the Bundela, about six *kos* from Narwar, and after a short but gallant resistance he fell dead, and his head was sent as an acceptable offering to the Prince. Early in the reign of Jahángír, the murderer received high promotion, and Jahángír in his Memoirs avows and justifies his having procured the murder by promise of reward. Akbar's grief at the death of his minister was unbounded, and he took active measures to bring Bír Singh to punishment. The murderer was hunted from place to place, and had several hair-breadth escapes; but the death of the Emperor put an end to his danger, and opened the road to reward and honour.

The author of the *Ma-ásiru-l Umará* writes as follows in his Memoirs:

"It has often been asserted that Abú-l Fazl was an infidel. Some say he was a Hindú, or a fire-worshipper, or a free thinker; and some go still further and call him an atheist; but others pass a juster sentence, and say that he was a pantheist, and that, like other *Súfis*, he claimed for himself a position above the law of the Prophet. There is no doubt that he was a man of lofty character, and desired to live at peace with all men. He never said anything improper. Abuse, stoppages of wages, fines, absence on the part of his servants, did not exist in his household. If he appointed a man whom he afterwards found to be useless, he did not remove him, but kept him as long as he could; for he used to say that, if he dismissed him, people would accuse him of want of penetration in having appointed an unsuitable agent. On the day when the sun entered Aries, he inspected his whole household and took stock, keeping the inventory with himself, and burning last year's books. He also gave his whole wardrobe to his servants, with the exception of his trousers, which were burnt in his presence.

"He had an extraordinary appetite. It is said that, exclusive of water and soup, he consumed daily twenty-two *sirs* of food. His son 'Abdu-r Rahmán used to sit at table as *safarchi* (head butler); the superintendent of the kitchen, who was a Muhammadan, was also in attendance, and both watched to see if Abú-l Fazl would eat twice of one and the same dish. If he did, the dish was sent up again the next day. If anything appeared tasteless, Abú-l Fazl gave it to his son to taste, and he to the superintendent, but no word was said about it. When Abú-l Fazl was in the Dakhin, his table luxury exceeded all belief. In an immense tent, 1000 rich dishes were daily served up and distributed among the *amirs*; and near it another large tent was pitched for all-comers to dine, whether rich or poor, and *khichri* was cooked all day, and was served out to any one that applied for it.

"As a writer, Abú-l Fazl stands unrivalled. His style is grand, and is free from the technicalities and flimsy prettiness of other *munshis*; and the force of his words, the structure of his sentences, the suitableness of his compounds, and the elegance of his periods, are such that it would be difficult for any one to imitate him."

Other native writers have expressed similar opinions, and Mr. Blochmann, to whom the above translation is owing, says, "It would be almost useless to add to this encomium on Abú-l Fazl's style. 'Abdu-lla, King of Bukhárá, said that he was more afraid of Abú-l Fazl's pen than of Akbar's arrow. Everywhere in India he is known as the great *munshi*. His letters are studied in all *madrasas*; and though a beginner may find them difficult and perplexing, they are perfect models. But a great familiarity, not only with the Persian language, but also with Abú-l Fazl's style, is required to make the reading of any of his works a pleasure. His composition stands unique, and though everywhere studied, he cannot be, and has not been, imitated." Yet attention may be called to the just criticism recorded by Ináyatu-llah, the author of the continuation of the *Akbar-náma*, who says that the later volumes of this work were considered more laboured and abstruse than the first.[1] The style is certainly more complicated and ambitious, and many unusual and even foreign words are employed, so that unwearied attention is required to seize and follow up the meaning of the author.

Abú-l Fazl was author of several works of repute. On his introduction to the Emperor, he presented a Commentary on a *Surat* of the Kurán, which he called *A'yatu-l Kúrsi*. But Badáúní does not fail to record that "people said it was written by his father." The *Maktúbátu-l 'Allámi*, more commonly called *Inshá-i Abú-l Fazl*, is a collection of letters written by Abú-l

[1] See *infrà* next Article.

Fazl to kings and chiefs. The *Ayár-i Dánish* is a translation of the Arabic *Kalila o Damna*. He was also the author of some smaller and less known works. The greatest of his productions was the *Akbar-náma*, in two volumes, and the *A'ín-i Akbarí*, which is considered to be its third volume. The *A'ín*, or Institutes, may, however, be regarded as a distinct work. A translation of it by Gladwin was published in the year 1800; but although a very meritorious production for the time, it was imperfect and often incorrect. The first volume of a new translation by Mr. Blochmann, of the Calcutta Madrasa, has just been published. It is a precise and admirable version, and is enriched with numerous notes, which testify to the deep learning and great research of their author. It includes also a series of memoirs of all the nobles and notable persons of Akbar's Court. When the work is complete, the translation will be well worthy to rank with the original. The purely historical part of the *Akbar-náma* comprises in the first volumes an account of the ancestors of Akbar from Tímúr to Bábar. It has a full history of the reign of Humáyún, of which a few Extracts will appear in the following pages. The history of the reign of Akbar is given in full, year by year, from the accession of the Emperor to the end of the forty-sixth year of the reign, A.D. 1602. Many Extracts have been taken from this part of the work.

The *Akbar-náma* enjoys a much higher reputation in India than in Europe. The passage above quoted from the *Ma-ásiru-l Umará* is a fair and temperate expression of Oriental judgment. Sir Henry Elliot, whose opinion coincides with that expressed by Elphinstone, and adopted by Morley, gives an unfavourable verdict. He says, "The authority of the *Akbar-náma* is not rated very high in Europe, and Abú-l Fazl is not for a moment to be compared, either in frankness or simplicity, with Comines, Sully, Clarendon and other ministers who have written contemporary history; for though he was a man of enlarged views and extraordinary talents, yet, as Elphinstone remarks, he was a professed rhetorician, and is still the model of the unnatural style which is so much admired in India. He was, besides, a most assiduous courtier, eager to extol the virtues, to gloss over the crimes, and to preserve the dignity of his master and those in whom he was interested. His dates and his general statements of events are valuable; but he requires constant attention, not so much to guard against his barefaced partiality, as against the prejudice which he draws on his favourites by his fawning and fulsome adulation of them, and against the suspicions which he excites by his dishonest way of telling a story, even in cases where the action related was innocent or excusable. His narrative is florid, feeble and indistinct, overloaded with commonplace reflections and pious effusions, generally ending in a compliment to his patron. 'Every event that had a tendency to take from his goodness, wisdom, or power, is passed over or mis-stated, and a uniform strain of panegyric and triumph is kept up, which disgusts the reader with the author, and almost with the hero. Amidst these unmeaning flourishes, the real merits of Akbar disappear, and it is from other authors that we learn the motives of his actions, the difficulties he had to contend with, and the resources by which they were surmounted. The gross flattery of a book written by one so well acquainted with Akbar's disposition, and submitted, it appears, to his own inspection, leaves an impression of the vanity of that prince, which is almost the only blot on his otherwise admirable character.'"[1]

A careful examination of the whole of the book, and the translating of many passages, compel the Editor of this work to withhold his assent from this unqualified condemnation. It is true that in certain passages Abú-l Fazl attributes to Akbar a prescience which approaches to prophecy and powers almost supernatural; but, as Price observes, his veneration for the Emperor amounted almost to adoration. Apart from these occasional blemishes, his faults are those of the rhetorician rather than of the flatterer, and his style ought to be judged by an Oriental standard, not by a contrast with the choicest of Euro-

[1] This is quoted from Elphinstone.

pean memoirs. But though the Editor had arrived at this judgment, he might have hesitated to express it here, had it not been confirmed by the independent opinion of a competent authority. In the preface to his *A'in-i Akbari* but just arrived in England, Mr. Blochmann says: "Abú-l Fazl has far too often been accused by European writers of flattery, and even of wilful concealment of facts damaging to the reputation of his master. A study of the *Akbar-náma* will show that the charge is absolutely unfounded; and if we compare his works with other historical productions of the East, we shall find that while he praises, he does so infinitely less, and with much more grace and dignity, than any other Indian historian or poet. No native writer has ever accused him of flattery; and if we bear in mind that all Eastern works on Ethics recommend unconditional assent to the opinion of the king, whether correct or absurd, as the whole duty of man, and that the whole poetry of the East is a rank mass of flattery, at the side of which modern encomiums look like withered leaves, we may pardon Abú-l Fazl when he praises because he finds a true hero."

Major Price has given, in his "Retrospect of Mahommedan History," a copious abstract of the *Akbar-náma* for the interval between Tímúr and Akbar. He has also translated elsewhere the account of the capture of Chítor. Major Stewart has translated the account of the taking of Surat. There is in MS. in the Library of the Royal Asiatic Society an abridged translation of the whole work by "Lieut. Chambers, of the Madras Army." This translation was used by Elphinstone for the purposes of his History; and the Editor of this work has had the benefit of it during a portion of the time that he has been at work upon the *Akbar-náma*. The translation of the Extracts which follow this have all been made by the Editor.

A lithographed edition of the *Akbar-náma*, in three quarto volumes, was printed at Lucknow in 1867, at the expense of the Rájá of Pattiála. It is a handsome and costly work, and it is greatly to be regretted that its literary value is by no means commensurate with the money expended upon it. Gross and obvious errors abound in it, and there are many passages wanting. In one instance the annals of six months of one of the most important years of the reign (the 17th) are altogether omitted. The Editor has used this edition, and it being the only one published, he has referred to it in the following Extracts. But his chief reliance has been on an excellent *Shikasta* MS. belonging to the Royal Asiatic Society. He has also had the use of a fair MS. belonging to the Library of the India Office, and of other volumes containing only portions of the work. A new edition of the work is promised for the Bibliotheca Indica.

The *Akbar-náma* has been translated into Hindústání by Muhammad Khalíl 'Alí Khán, under the name of *Wáki'át-i Akbari*.[1]]

EXTRACTS.

Reign of the Emperor Humáyún.

Kálinjar.

(See Vol. V. p. 189.)

[Text, vol. i. p. 152.] Five or six months after (his accession), Humáyún marched to subdue the fort of Kálinjar. He had invested the place nearly a month, when the garrison being reduced to distress, the commander (*hákim*) submitted. He gave twelve *mans* of gold, besides other things, as tribute, and the Emperor, acceding to his entreaties and lamentations, forgave him, and marched away towards the fort of Chunár, with the intention of besieging that fortress.

Rebellion of the Mirzás.

(See Vol. V. p. 189.)

[Text, vol. i. p. 153.] (In the year 940 H., 1533-4 A.D.), Muhammad Zamán Mirzá, Muhammad Sultán Mirzá, with his son

[1] [The materials for this notice have been derived by the Editor from memoranda left by Sir H. Elliot, and from the valuable Memoir of Abú-l Fazl by Mr. Blochmann, printed as an Introduction to his translation of the *Áín-i Akbari*. To that Memoir the reader is referred for further details. See also Morley's *Cat. of the MSS. of the Royal Asiatic Society*.]

Ulugh Mirzá, broke out in rebellion, and Humáyún marched against them. He encamped at Bhojpúr, by the side of the Ganges, and sent Yádgár Násir Mirzá over the river at the head of a force against the rebels. Yádgár attacked them, gained a victory, and took Muhammad Zamán Mirzá, Muhammad Sultán Mirzá, and Walí Khub Mirzá prisoners. Muhammad Zamán Mirzá was sent prisoner to Bayána, the other two persons were blinded and sent away in disgrace. Muhammad Zamán Mirzá, unmindful of the mercy shown him, pretended to be submissive, and, effecting his escape, fled to Sultán Bahádur, of Gujarát.

Prince Kámrán gets possession of Lahore.

(See Vol. V. p. 189.)

[Text, vol. i. p. 153.] When Prince Kámrán heard of the death of the Emperor Bábar, he left Kandahár in charge of Mirzá 'Askarí, and set off for Hindústán, to see how he might advance his own interests. At that time Mír Yúnas 'Alí, who had been appointed by the late Emperor, was governor of Lahore. Mirzá Kámrán revolved in his mind a scheme for getting hold of Lahore. One night he falsely pretended to have a difference with Karácha Beg, and spoke harshly to him, so that Karácha Beg left the camp of the Mirzá with his soldiers, and went off to Lahore. Mír Yúnas 'Alí was glad of his coming, and showed him much attention; frequently inviting him to his house, and enjoying his society. Karácha Beg watched his opportunity, and one night when they were drinking wine, and the Mír's soldiers were gone to their homes, Karácha Beg seized him, put him in confinement, and placed his own men in charge of the gates of the fortress. He then sent a messenger to call Mirzá Kámrán, who was expecting such a summons, and starting off with expedition, gained possession of Lahore. He took Mír Yúnas out of prison, and offered to make over the government of Lahore to him; but the Mír declined to accept it, and went to the Emperor Humáyún.

Mirzá Kámrán appointed his own officers over the *parganas* of the Panjáb, as far as the Satlej or river of Ludhiyána. He sent envoys to the Emperor, assuring him of his good intentions, and asking to be confirmed in the government. Humáyún, in his kindness, consented, and recognized him as governor of Kábul, Kandahár, and the Panjáb. * * * In the year 933 Mirzá Kámrán removed Mirzá 'Askarí from the government of Kandahár, and gave it to Khwája Kalán Beg, being annoyed with 'Askarí in consequence of his having been worsted in a fight with the Hazáras while on his way to Kábul.

March against Bengal.

(See Vol. V. p. 190.)

[Text, vol. i. p. 155.] In the year 941 Humáyún turned his attention to the conquest of the eastern countries, and marched to subdue Bengal. When he arrived at the town of Kinár, near Kálpí, he was informed that Sultán Bahádur of Gujarát had laid siege to the fort of Chítor, and had detached a large force under the command of Tátár Khán, who had very ambitious projects in his head; so in the month of Jumáda-l awwal Humáyún fell back to resist his enemies.

Tátár Khán pressed his delusive advice upon Sultán Bahádur, and strongly urged that he might be sent towards the Imperial dominions, representing Humáyún's army to be given up to pleasure and indolence. Sultán Bahádur took measures to forward the views of the rebels. Having fitted out Tátár Khán, he sent twenty *krors* of the old Gujarát coinage,[1] equal to forty of the ordinary Dehlí standard,[2] to the fort of Rantambhor, there to be expended by Tátár Khán in raising forces. He sent Sultán 'Aláu-d dín, father of Tátár Khán,[3] in command of a strong force, against Kálinjar, to increase the rebellious feeling in that neighbourhood. Burhánu-l Mulk Bunyání was sent with a force

[1] زرقديم گجرات. [2] معمول دهلي.

[3] ['Aláu-d dín was brother to Sultán Sikandar Lodí, and uncle of Sultán Ibráhím. —*Text.*]

of Gujarátís through Nágor, to make a demonstration against the Panjáb. Under the idea that the Imperial army would now disperse, he divided his own army, and although wise and experienced counsellors advised him to keep his army together, their words had no effect. When Tátár Kkán marched on his wild enterprise against Dehlí, Sultán Bahádur himself proceeded to invest the fort of Chítor. * * * Tátár Khán, employing the money at his disposal, gathered a force of nearly forty thousand horse, of Afgháns and others, with which he advanced and took Bayána. While this was going on, Humáyún was engaged in his invasion of the east country; but on receiving the intelligence of it, he hastened back to Ágra. Mirzás 'Askarí and Hindál and Yádgár Násir Mirzá and * * * were sent with eighteen thousand horse to meet the chief army of insurgents, which was marching against Dehlí, for it was deemed expedient to defeat this army first. When the Imperial army approached the insurgents, numbers of the latter deserted every day, until the force dwindled down to three thousand horse. The men collected with so much trouble, and at so great an expense, had neither the heart to advance nor the spirit to fight. At length he (Tátár Khán), washing his hands of life, fought with all the strength he could muster, at Mandráil, and was there killed.

Campaign against Sultán Bahádur.

(See Vol. V. p. 190.)

[Text, vol. i. p. 159.] Humáyún left Ágra on his expedition against Gujarát, in the beginning of Jumáda-l awwal, 941 H. When he encamped near the fort of Ráisín, the commandant sent large presents with a message, saying that the fort was His Majesty's, and the men of the garrison were the servants of His Majesty, and they would hold the fort till Sultán Bahádur's business was settled. As the Emperor was intent upon the conquest of Gujarát, he did not delay here, but marched on to Málwa, and encamped at Sárangpúr. Sultán Bahádur was engaged in the siege of Chítor; and when he heard of the

Emperor's advance, he held a council with his officers, the majority of whom were for raising the siege, and marching against the Emperor. But Sadr Khán, a wise and prudent councillor, urged that the fort was upon the point of surrender, and that they should press the siege to a conclusion, for no Muhammadan king would attack while they were engaged in war with infidels. This advice was followed, and on the 3rd Ramazán, 941 H., the fort of Chítor was taken.

Flight of Bahádur.

(See Vol. V. p. 192.)

[Text, vol. i. p. 162.] On the 21st of Shawwál Sultán Bahádur lost all hope. He ordered all the large guns and mortars to be filled with powder, and to be fired till they burst. When night came on, he, along with Mírán Muhammad Shujá' and five or six of his personal associates, went out from the back of the camp towards Ágra, and afterwards turned towards Mandú. Sadr Khán and 'Imádu-l Mulk went off with 20,000 horse direct to Mandú, and Muhammad Zamán Mirzá with another body went off towards Lahore, to raise disturbances. Great cries and clamour arose on that night from the Gujarátí camp; but the facts of the matter were not known to the Imperial army. The Emperor mounted and remained under arms till morning. It was not till one watch of the day had passed, that Sultán Bahádur's flight became known. The troops then entered the camp, and obtained great plunder. Khudáwand Khán, the tutor and minister of Sultán Bahádur, was taken prisoner. He was very graciously treated, and taken into the Emperor's service. Yádgár Násir Mirzá, Kásim Sultán, and Hindú Beg were sent in pursuit of the fugitives. * * * Sadr Khán and 'Imádu-l Mulk went straight to Mandú, and Humáyún followed, and encamped before the fort. Rúmí Khán deserted from the Gujarátís, and came in to the Emperor, who bestowed a robe upon him. On the 14th (?), Sultán Bahádur entered the fort, and the question of peace came to be debated, and it was proposed that Gujarát and Chítor should remain in the hands of Sultán Bahádur, and that Mandú should be given up to the Emperor. These terms were finally agreed upon by the negociators on both sides. But on that night the garrison of the fort relaxed their guard, and a party of about two hundred soldiers of the Imperial army went to the back of the fortress, and scaled the walls by means of ladders and ropes. Jumping down from the walls, they opened the gate, and brought in their horses, and others followed. Mallú Khán, the commander of the batteries, a native of Mandú, who had the title of Kádir Sháhí, learnt what was passing, seized a horse, and went to Sultán Bahádur. He was asleep, but the cries of Mallú Khán aroused him, and he rushed out with three or four attendants. On his way he met Bhúpat Rái, son of Silhadi, one of his councillors, with about twenty horse, whom he joined. On reaching the gate at the top of the *maidán*, they encountered a party of about 200 of the Imperial cavalry. Sultán Bahádur was the first to attack them. He was followed by some others, and he cut his way through, and went off with Mallú Khán and another attendant to the fort of Súngar.[1] He had his horses let down (the precipice of the town) by ropes. He himself followed through a thousand difficulties, and took the road to Gujarát. Kásim Husain Khán (an Imperial officer) was stationed near the fort, and an Uzbek servant of his, named Borí, who had previously been in Sultán Bahádur's service, recognized his old master, and told Kásim Husain, but he took no notice of it. So Sultán Bahádur escaped to Chámpanír, being joined on the way by about 1,500 men.

Return of Humáyún from Gujarát.

(See Vol. V. p. 193.)

[Text, vol. i. p. 172.] [After the conquest of Ahmadábád and] the settlement of the affairs of Gujarát, Humáyún marched towards the port of Díú (in pursuit of Sultán Bahádur); but

[1] "The citadel of Mandú,"—*suprà*, Vol. V. p. 192.

when he left Dandúka, which is about thirty *kos* from Ahmadábád, letters reached him from Agra with the information that affairs had gone on badly since his departure from the capital, and that revolts had broken out in several quarters. News also came from Málwa, that Sikandar Khán and Mallú Khán had risen and attacked Mihtar Zambúr, the *jágírdár* of Hindia, who had removed into Ujjain with his property. The troops stationed at various places in the province had also gone into Ujjain, where they were besieged by the insurgents. Darwesh 'Alí, *Kitábdár*, the governor, was killed by a gunshot, and the garrison then capitulated. This intelligence determined Humáyún to fall back, and to take up his residence for a time at Mandú, whilst he cleared the province of Málwa of rebels, settled the affairs of the conquered country of Gujarát, and suppressed the revolts in the vicinity of the capital. He therefore placed Gujarát in charge of Mirzá 'Askarí.

Sultán Bahádur recovers Gujarát.

(See Vol. V. p. 197.)

[Text, vol. i. p. 173.] Nearly three months had passed after the Emperor's departure, when the enemy drew together and commenced operations. Khán Jahán Shírází and Rúmí Khán, whose name was Safar, and who was the builder of the fort of Surat, operated in concert. They took possession of Nausárí, which was held by 'Abdu-lla Khán, an officer of Husain Khán, and he retired to Broach. About the same time they took Surat. Khán Jahán then marched against Broach, and Rúmí Khán embarked his guns and muskets (*tufang*) in war *ghrábs*, and proceeded thither by water. Kásim Husain (the governor), unable to make any resistance, went to Chámpanír, and from thence he proceeded to Ahmadábád, seeking help from Mirzá 'Askarí, and Hindú Beg. Saiyid Ishák, who had received from Sultán Bahádur the title of Shitáb Khán, took possession of Kambay. Yádgár Násir Mirzá was summoned from Pattan to Ahmadábád by Mirzá 'Askarí. Daryá Khán and Muháfiz Khán, who were proceeding from Ráisín to Sultán Bahádur at Díú, finding Pattan deserted, took possession of it.

Retreat of Mirzá 'Askari from Ahmadábád.

(See Vol. V. p. 197.)

[Text, vol. i. p. 174.] When Mirzá 'Askarí retired from Ahmadábád, Sultán Bahádur was full of misgiving and anxiety, but this gave him courage. He pursued the retreating forces, and on coming up with them, Yádgár Násir Mirzá, who was in command of the rear-guard, turned upon him. A sharp fight ensued, in which many of Bahádur's advanced force were killed or taken prisoners. Sultán Bahádur then stopped at Mahmudábád, and the Mirzá rejoined his army. Mirzá 'Askarí had given up all idea of fighting, and continued his march. He lost a good many men in crossing the Mahindarí, whither Sultán Bahádur followed him.

Mirzá 'Askari at Chámpanir.

(See Vol. V. p. 198.)

[Text, vol. i. p. 175.] When the Mirzás arived at Chámpanír, Tardí Beg Khán received them hospitably, and then retired to his own abode. Next day the Mirzás, with evil designs, sent a message to him, representing the distressed condition of themselves and their army, and asking him to give them some money out of the treasures of the fort. This would enable them to turn and face the enemy, and to communicate with (Humáyún at) Mandú, which a messenger might do in six days. Tardí Beg did not accede to their request. The Mirzás then resolved to seize him, to take possession of all the treasures, and to proclaim Mirzá 'Askarí king. They would then endeavour to make terms with Sultán Bahádur, and if unsuccessful, they would march towards Ágra, which had been left unprotected by Humáyún, because he preferred the climate of Málwa. Tardí Beg came out of the fort to wait upon the Mirzás; but on his way he received information of their designs, and hastened back into the fort. He then sent to tell the Mirzás that they must not stay there, and they replied that they were going, and wished him to come and say farewell. But he knew their object, and sent a suitable answer. Next morning Tardí Beg fired a gun (to show that he was ready to fight), and the Mirzás marched off by way of Ghát-Karjí, in execution of their wild plan against Ágra. Whilst they remained at Chámpanír, Sultán Bahádur did not cross the Mahindarí, which is about fifteen *kos* distant. But when he heard of their march towards Ágra, and of the foolish scheme they had formed, he crossed the river, and advanced against Chámpanír. Notwithstanding the strength of the fort, and its abundance of munitions, Tardí Beg evacuated the fortress, and went to Humáyún at Mandú, where he informed him of all the Mirzás' evil designs.

Rebellion of Muhammad Sultán Mirzá and Ulugh Mirzá.

(See Vol. V. p. 198.)

[Text, vol. i. p. 176.] One of the disgraceful proceedings which recalled Humáyún to Ágra was the rebellion of Sultán Mirzá and Ulugh Mirzá his son. It has already been related how they before rebelled, and how an order was given to deprive them of sight. But the party entrusted with this order did not execute it, and they escaped. They now again commenced their rebellious proceedings, and after attacking Bilgrám, they went to Kanauj, which was held by the sons of Khusrú Kokaltásh. These men surrendered, and were replaced in charge of Kanauj. Mirzá Hindál, who was in Ágra, went out against them, and crossing the Ganges near Bilgrám, the armies met, and a battle ensued, in which the rebels were defeated. Hindál pursued, and overtook them at Oudh, where Ulugh Beg and his sons were assembled and ready to fight again. The news of the Emperor's return from Gujarát to Ágra now arrived, and the rebels fought once more, and were defeated. Hindál then returned victorious to Ágra.

Death of Sultán Bahádur.

[Text, vol. i. p. 177.] When Humáyún returned to Ágra, Bhúpál Rái, the ruler of Bíjágarh,[1] finding the fort of Mandú empty, came up boldly and took possession of it. Kádir Sháh also returned there, and Mírán Muhammad Fárúkí also came up from Burhánpúr. Sultán Bahádur remained a fortnight at Chámpanír, and then returned to Díú. * * Upon reaching the port, he found the Portuguese commander had arrived there with his vessels and fighting men. The Portuguese chief was apprehensive that as the Sultán was no longer in want of assistance, he meditated some treachery. So he sent to inform the Sultán that he had come as requested, but that he was ill and unable to go on shore, so that the interview must be deferred until he got better. The Sultán, quitting the royal road of safety, proceeded on the 3rd Ramazán, 943 H., with a small escort, on board a boat to visit the Governor. As soon as he reached the vessel, he discovered that it was a mere pretence of sickness, and he was sorry that he had come. He sought to return directly; but the Portuguese were unwilling that such prey should escape them, and hoped that by keeping him prisoner, they might obtain some more ports. The governor came forward, and asked the Sultán to stay a little while, and examine some curiosities he had to present. The Sultán requested that they might be sent after him, and turned quickly towards his own boat. A European *kázi* (priest?) placed himself in the Sultán's way, and bade him stop. The Sultán, in exasperation, drew his sword, and cleft him in twain; then he leaped into his own boat. The Portuguese vessels which were around drew together round the Sultán's boat, and a fight began. The Sultán and Rúmí Khán threw themselves into the water. A friend among the Portuguese stretched a hand to Rúmí Khán, and saved him; but the Sultán was drowned in the waves. His companions also perished.

[1] Sixty miles south of Mandú.

Humáyún's march to Bengal.

(See Vol. V. p. 199.)

[Text, vol. i. p. 184.] When the Emperor arrived at Patna, part of his army having come by water, part by land, his counsellors advised him to delay his campaign till after the rainy season. * * * But the King of Bengal urged expedition, and Humáyún complied. When he arrived at Bhágalpúr, he divided his army, and sent Mirzá Hindál, with 5000 men, over the river to march on that side. On reaching Mungír, Humáyún found that Sher Khán had left his son Jalál Khán, afterwards Salím Khán (Sháh), with Khawáss Khán, and * * with 15,000 men, in charge of the town of Garhí, which is the gate of Bengal, and had himself gone to Jhárkand.[1] * * When the Imperial army reached Garhí, Jalál Khán, disregarding his father's commands, came out and attacked them, * and defeated them. * * Humáyún then hastened forward, and the Afgháns abandoned the place and fled.

Progress of Sher Sháh.

(See Vol. V. p. 200.)

[Text, vol. i. p. 186.] [While Humáyún was at Gaur] Sher Khán seized the opportunity to increase his power. He besieged Benares, and in a short time got possession of the place, and killed the governor, Mír Fazalí. From thence he marched against Jaunpúr, which was held by Bábá Beg Jaláír, father of Sháham Khán, who had been appointed after the death of Hindú Beg. He set the defences of the place in order, and was joined from Oudh by Yúsuf Beg, son of Ibráhím Beg, who was on the march to Bengal. Yúsuf Beg scoured the neighbourhood with his patrols, and was eager for the fray. Jalál Khán, hearing of this, made a rapid march with 2000 men. When Yusúf Beg came in sight of this force, he at once prepared for battle. He was strongly dissuaded by his officers, on account of the great

[1] Called *Chahárkand* in the text.

disparity of the two forces, but he would not listen. After fighting bravely, he was killed, and next day the enemy invested Jaunpúr. Bábá Beg Jaláír exerted himself strenuously in its defence, and wrote to the *mirzás* and the *amírs*, as well as to the Emperor, to inform them of his position.

Sher Sháh occupies Bengal.

(See Vol. V. p. 204.)

[Text, vol. i. p. 194.] [After the battle of Chaunsá], Sher Khán resolved upon getting possession of Bengal, and marched as far as the frontier of Bihár. There he stopped, and sent his son Jalál Khán with a detachment on this expedition. In a short time he met Jahángír Kulí Beg,[1] and the latter fought bravely. But the decrees of fate were against him, and the *amirs* of Bengal did not show proper spirit in opposing the rebels. Fond of their ease, they rendered no support to Jahángír Kulí. Unable to succeed in the field, Jahángír Kulí sought refuge with the *zamíndárs*, and he and many of his followers were killed. At ease as to Bengal, Sher Khán advanced, and got possession of Jaunpúr. He then sent his younger son Kutb Khán against Kálpí and Etáwa.

Humáyún's bridge over the Ganges.

(See Vol. IV., and Vol. V. p. 205.)

[Text, vol. i. p. 198.] When Humáyún reached Bhojpúr, he found Sher Khán encamped with a large army on the other side of the Ganges. The Emperor ordered a bridge to be thrown over, and it was soon constructed at the ferry of Bhojpúr. * * The Afgháns brought up the elephant Gard-báz, which they had taken at the battle of Chaunsá, to destroy the bridge, and the elephant pressed against the head of the bridge and brought it down. * * It was now thought advisable to march along the bank of the river to Kanauj.

[1] Governor of Bengal, appointed by Humáyún.

Reign of the Emperor Akbar.

Famine.

(See Vol. V. p. 247.)

[Text, vol. ii. p. 42.] At this time (first year of the reign of Akbar), there was a great scarcity in Hindústán. In some districts, and especially in the province of Dehlí, it reached a most alarming height. If men could find money, they could not get sight of corn. Men were driven to the extremity of eating each other, and some formed themselves into parties to carry off lone individuals for their food.

Destruction of Hímú's family.—Alwar and Ajmír.

(See Vol. V. p. 253.)

[Text, vol. ii. p. 56.] Akbar was now informed that Hájí Khán, a *ghulám* of Sher Khán Afghán [Sher Sháh], a brave and able general, was setting up pretensions to rule in Alwar, and that Hímú's father and wife, and all his property and wealth, were in that country. So the Emperor sent Násiru-l Mulk [Pír Muhammad Sarwání] with a select force to attack him. Hájí Khán, in dread of the Imperial army, fled before it arrived. Alwar and all the territory of Mewát thus came into the Imperial power. The fugitives proceeded to Dewatí-májárí, a strong place, which was Hímú's family home. Much resistance and fighting followed. Hímú's father was taken alive, and brought before Násiru-l Mulk, who tried to convert him to the faith; but the old man said, "For eighty years I have worshipped God in the way of my own religion; how can I now forsake my faith? Shall I, through fear of death, embrace your religion without understanding it?" Mauláná Pír Muhammad treated his question as unheard, but gave him an answer with the tongue of the sword. He then returned with much spoil and fifty elephants to the Emperor. Hájí Khán, when he left Alwar, proceeded to Ajmír, deeming that a secure refuge for his family, and prepared his soldiers for battle. The Ráná, who was a great *zamíndár*, was the son of that *ráná* who had acted improperly towards the late Emperor Humáyún, and had suffered defeat at his hands. Hájí Khán made demands upon him, and grievously troubled him, so that a battle was fought between them in the vicinity of Ajmír. Hájí Khán and Muzaffar Khán Sarwání, his *vakil*, exhibited conspicuous gallantry in the fight, and the Ráná, who was too confident in the number of his forces, was defeated. Hájí Khán then took possession of Ajmír and Nágor and all those parts. When this success of Hájí Khán's was reported to the Emperor, he appointed Saiyid Muhammad Kásim Khán Naishapúrí and * * to march against him. * * * Intelligence was now brought that Hájí Khán was so strong as to offer resistance to the forces sent against him; so the Emperor determined to proceed to Hisár, and to send reinforcements from thence. After visiting the tomb of his father at Sirhind, he proceeded to Hisár, accompanied by Bairám Khán. * * * When intelligence of this reached Hájí Khán, his forces dispersed. Every man went to his own place, and Hájí Khán himself hastened to Gujarát. Muhammad Kásim Khán was sent by the Emperor to take charge of Ajmír. Saiyid Muhammad Bárha and Sháh Kulí Khán Mahram were sent out with a force to capture Jítasáran, and they killed a great many Rájpúts, and made themselves masters of the fort.

Second Year of the Reign.

Death of 'Adali.

(See Vol. IV. p. 508.)

[Text, vol. ii. p. 72.] The son of Muhammad Khán, ruler of Bengal, Sadar Khán[1] by name, but who had assumed the title of Jalálu-d dín, resolved to take his revenge on Mubáriz Khán ('Adalí) for having caused the death of his father on the field of battle. He accordingly marched against Mubáriz Khán, and overthrew and slew him in a great battle. He had reigned four years and some days.

[1] *Sic*—"Khizr Khán" was the real name.

THIRD YEAR OF THE REIGN.

Adham Khán at Hathkánt.

(See Vol. V. p. 256.)

[Text, vol. ii. p. 97.] Among the transactions of this year was the appointment of Adham Khán with a body of men against Hathkánt,[1] which was the strongest place in the neighbourhood of Ágra. The *zamíndárs* of this place were Bhadauriyas[2] and others, and were remarkable for their numbers and courage. They were continually in rebellion against the Kings of Hindústán. Bairám Khán, having a rooted mistrust of Adham Khán, resolved to confer Hathkánt upon him in *jágír*; thus at once removing him from Court, and providing for the chastisement of the malcontents of that neighbourhood.

FOURTH YEAR OF THE REIGN.

Fall of Bairám Khán.

(See Vol. V. p. 261.)

[Text, vol. ii. p. 112.] Bairám Khán had been appointed by Humáyún tutor of his son Akbar, and the youth had often addressed him, as noble youths are accustomed to address their seniors, by the name "Bábá." The Emperor was now mindful of the fact, and overlooked in consequence many of Bairám's unseemly actions. * * But at length Bairám's proceedings went beyond all endurance, and he formed some sinister designs in conspiracy with evil-minded flatterers like Wali Beg Zú-l Kadr and Shaikh Gadáí Kambú. When the Emperor became acquainted with the evil designs of these conspirators, he communicated them, before they could be carried into execution, to some of his devoted and intelligent advisers, such as Máham Ánka, remarkable for her intelligence, judgment, and sincerity, to Adham Khán, Mirzá Sharfu-d dín Husain, and some others. * * The Emperor crossed over to Bayána on a hunting excursion, and

[1] On the left bank of the Chambal.—See Glossary, vol. i. p. 86; vol. ii. p. 26.
[2] Ib., vol. ii. p. 25.

Máham Ánka then made known the facts to Shahábu-d dín Ahmad Khán, the governor of Dehlí, a man distinguished for his judgment, shrewdness, and fidelity. * * * The first person of distinction who deserted Bairám Khán was Kiyá Khán Gang, an old and faithful servant of the throne. After that others fell off, one by one and two by two, and proceeded to Court. Máham Ánka, in accord with Shahábu-d dín Ahmad Khán, communicated all important matters to His Majesty, and became responsible for the discharge of the duties of the minister. * * * As a political expedient, and for the public discharge of business, Máham Ánka recommended Bahádur Khán, brother of 'Alí Kulí Khán, for the exalted office of minister, and His Majesty appointed him. * * But although he received Etáwa in *jágír*, and bore the name of minister, the real duties were discharged by Máham Ánka.

Fifth Year of the Reign.

Character of Bairám Khán.

[Text, vol. ii. p. 164.] Bairám's natural character was good and amiable. But through bad company, that worst misfortune of man, his natural good qualities were overclouded, and arrogance was fostered by flattery. Every one who looks with complacency on his own merits and deserts opens his heart to the wiles of sycophants.

Sixth Year of the Reign.

Adham Khán.

(See Vol. V. p. 271.)

[Text, vol. ii. p. 181.] The folly and wilfulness of Adham Khán were well known. His mother, Máham Ánka, had charge of the royal harem, and he now conspired with some of his mother's servants to carry off two of the beauties of Báz Bahádur, who had lately been presented to the Emperor. When every one was engaged in preparing for the march, and little heed was paid to what was going on, the abduction was effected. When this disgraceful action was made known to the Emperor, he sent two fast riders after the fugitives, who exerted themselves so well that they overtook them, and brought them back. Máham Ánka, lest these two women should be brought into the presence of the Emperor, and expose her conduct and the villany of her son, had the two poor innocent girls put to death, for dead people tell no tales. His Majesty had not yet torn the veil from his eyes, so he passed over this heinous crime.

SEVENTH YEAR OF THE REIGN.

Prisoners of War not to be made Slaves.

[Text, vol. ii. p. 202.] One of the gracious acts of His Majesty in this (seventh) year of his reign was the prohibition against making slaves of prisoners taken in war. It had been the custom of the royal troops, in their victorious campaigns in India, to forcibly sell or keep in slavery the wives, children, and dependents of the natives. But His Majesty, actuated by his religious, prudent, and kindly feelings, now issued an order that no soldier of the royal army should act in this manner; for although evil-disposed men might follow senseless courses, and taking up arms against the Emperor might suffer defeat, the children and people belonging to them were to be secure from all molestation from the royal troops, and no one, small or great, was to be made a slave. All were to be free to go as they pleased to their own houses or to the houses of their relatives; for although the repression and destruction of insolent opponents and the chastisement and coercion of rebels are among the duties of the ruling power, and are approved by lawyers and men of justice, still the punishment of their innocent wives and children is a transgression of the law. For if the husband pursues an evil course, what fault is it of the wife? and if the father rebels, how can the children be blamed?

Murder of Shamsu-d dín Muhammad Atka by Adham Khán.

(See Vol. V. p. 277.)

[Text, vol. ii. p. 218.] Adham Khán, the youngest son of that pattern of chastity Máham Ánka, who had neither a well-ordered mind nor a good temper, in the rashness of youth and intoxication of prosperity, was very envious of Shamsu-d dín Atka Khán. The Khán-khánán Mun'im Khán was also under the influence of the same feeling, and exhibited it constantly in ways that no one of lower dignity could have done. He irritated and excited Adham Khán, until at last, on the 12th Ramazán, a great outrage was committed. Mun'im Khán, Atka Khán, Shahábu-d dín Ahmad Khán, and other nobles, were sitting in the royal audience chamber engaged in business of state. Adham Khán came violently in with a party of ruffians more violent than himself. Those who were present in the court rose up, to show their respect, and Atka Khán also half stood up. As soon as he entered, Adham Khán clapped his hand to his dagger in a menacing way, and faced Atka Khán. He then cast an angry look upon Khusham Uzbek, one of his officers, and upon the other graceless wretches who had joined him in this outrageous business, as if to ask them why they hesitated. The truculent Khusham Uzbek then drew his dagger, and inflicted a terrible wound in the bosom of the minister. Atka Khán, in the greatest terror, rushed off towards the apartments of the Emperor, and had nearly reached them, when he received two sword cuts, and fell dead in the court yard of the palace. Dismay came upon all present, and a great outcry arose.

The blood-stained murderer, with that demented presumption which marked his proceedings, now directed his steps to the private apartments where His Majesty was sleeping. He mounted, sword in hand, to the parapet (*suffah*) which surrounds the palace on all sides about the height of a man and a half, and endeavoured to force his way inside. A eunuch who was near shut the door and locked it, and refused to open it for all the menaces of the assassin. The attendants of the royal court were greatly to be blamed that they did not at once inflict merited punishment on the murderer, and put a stop to his proceedings. But this want of resolution was probably ordained so that the courage and justice of the Emperor might become manifest to all, both small and great. The noise awoke him, and he inquired what was the matter, but no one of the inside attendants could inform him. He then went out himself to ascertain the facts. One of the old officers of the palace made known what had happened.

Amazed at the horrible statement, His Majesty inquired what it all meant, and the attendant then confirmed his words by pointing to the blood-stained corpse. When the Emperor realized the actual state of affairs, his anger blazed forth, and by a sudden inspiration he rushed out by another door, and not by that to which the assassin had fled in his vain hope. As he went forth, one of his attendants placed a sword in his hand without being asked for it. He took it and went on. On turning a corner of the parapet, he perceived the ungrateful culprit. Addressing him by an opprobrious epithet,[1] he asked what he had done. The presumptuous villain then rushed forward, and seizing both the hands of the Emperor, besought him to inquire into and reflect upon the matter, and not to condemn him without investigation. The Emperor, letting go his sword, delivered himself from the grasp of the culprit, and endeavoured to seize his sword. But the wretched man loosed his hold of the Emperor, and endeavoured to retain his sword. Relinquishing his attempt to get the sword, the Emperor struck him a blow in the face with his fist, which brought him senseless to the ground. Farhat Khán and Sangrám Hoshnak were there present, and the Emperor with angry looks demanded why they stood there looking on. He ordered them to bind the mad-brained fellow, and they and some others did so. He then gave his just command for them to cast him down headlong from the parapet. These stupid men

[1] *Bacha-i lddah*, "son of a bitch."

showed tenderness where want of tenderness would have been a thousand times better, and did not hurl him down as they ought to have done, and he was only half killed. They were then ordered to bring him up and cast him down again. So they dragged him back by the hair, and throwing him down more carefully, his neck was broken and his brains knocked out. So that criminal received the just reward of his deed. The vigorous hand of the Emperor had dealt him such a blow that those who were not aware of the fact supposed it to have been given with a mace.

Mun'im Khán Khán-khánán and Shahábu-d dín Ahmad Khán, who were near at hand, recoiled before the Emperor's anger, and took to flight. Yúsuf Muhammad Khán, the eldest son of Atka Khán, when he was informed of the fate of his father, assembled the Atka *khail* in arms, and blocked the road against Adham Khán and Máham Ánka. They were as yet unaware of the just retribution inflicted by His Majesty, who had paid no regard to his connection (*nisbat*) with Máham Ánka. * * But one of their number went and saw the punishment the culprit had received at the hands of the Emperor, and their anger was then appeased.

Máham Ánka was at her own home, stretched upon the bed of sickness. She had heard of her son's outrageous conduct, and that the Emperor had put him in confinement. Moved by her maternal affection, she arose and went to the Emperor, hoping to obtain the release of her son. When the Emperor saw her, he told her that Adham had killed his *atka*, and that he had inflicted the retaliatory punishment. Máham Ánka did not understand from this that her son was dead, so she replied that His Majesty had done well. But the *takhta-begi*, one of the ladies of the Court, then told her the truth, that he had been killed, and that he bore upon his face the marks of a blow with a mace,—these marks being, in fact, those made by His Majesty's fist.

Máham Ánka's good sense so far restrained her that she said nothing disrespectful to the Emperor, but she was greatly distressed. Her heart received a thousand wounds, and the colour forsook her face. She wished to go and see the body of her son, but His Majesty would not allow her, and he endeavoured to console and comfort her with kind and gentle words. On the same day the two corpses were sent to Dehlí, and the Emperor, after doing his utmost to console Máham Ánka, gave her permission to return home. That wise and grief-stricken woman respectfully took her departure. She then resigned herself to the divine decree, and passed her days in grief and sorrow. The disease with which she was afflicted increased, and forty days afterwards she died. His Majesty was deeply grieved at the death of this pattern of chastity. Her body was sent to Dehlí with all respect and honour, and the Emperor himself followed it for some steps. The nobles and officers of the state all testified their respect, and the Emperor ordered a splendid monument to be erected over her and her son.

Eighth Year of the Reign.

Remission of the Pilgrim Tax.

[Text, vol. ii. p. 239.] It was an old standing custom for the rulers of Hindústán to exact contributions, according to their respective means, from the pilgrims who visited the holy shrines. This tax was called *karmi.* His Majesty's judgment and equity condemned this exaction, and he remitted it, although it amounted to *krors* of rupees. An order was accordingly issued abolishing it throughout his dominions. * * * He was pleased to say that although this was a tax on the vain superstitions of the multitude, and the devotees did not pay it except when they travelled abroad, still the course they adopted was their mode of worshipping the Almighty, and the throwing of a stumbling-block and obstacle in their way could never be acceptable in the sight of God.

Ninth Year of the Reign.

Remission of the Jizya.

[Text, vol. ii. p. 257.] One of the munificent acts of the Emperor at the beginning of this the ninth year of his reign was the remission of the *jisya* (poll-tax upon infidels), which, in a country so extensive as Hindústán, amounted to an immense sum.

Conquest of Garha-katanka.

(See Vol. V. p. 288.)

[Text, vol. ii. p. 263.] Khwája 'Abdu-l Majíd Ásaf Khán, although he was a Tájik and a civilian, yet by the help of the good fortune of the Emperor, he had performed such deeds as would have humbled even Turks in his presence. He now resolved upon attempting the conquest of Garha-katanka. In the vast territories of Hindústán there is a country called Gondwána, that is, the land inhabited by the tribe of Gonds, —a numerous race of people, who dwell in the wilds, and pass most of their time in eating and drinking and the procreation of children. They are a very low race, and are held in contempt by the people of Hindústán, who look upon them as outcasts from their religion and laws. To the east of this country lies Ratanpúr, a dependency of the country of Jhárkand; and on the west it borders on Ráisín, belonging to the province of Málwa. The length of this district is 150 *kos*. On the north lies Panna,[1] and on the south the Dakhin, and the breadth is eighty *kos*. This country is called Garha-katanka, and it contains many strongholds and lofty forts. It has numerous towns and villages, and veracious writers have recorded that it contains seventy thousand villages. Garha is the name of the chief city, and Katanka is the name of a place[2] (near it), and these two places have given their names to the whole country. The seat of government was the fort of Chaurágarh.

In former times there was no one supreme ruler, but the country was ruled by several *rájás* and *ráis*, and at the present time, when, by the will of fortune, it no longer belongs to this

[1] This name is written "Patta" both in the print and in the MS., but the description given applies to Panna. Shaikh Illah-dád also writes it "Pattah" in his *Akbar-náma*.

[2] *mauza*, "place" or "village."

race, there are several *rájás*, such as Rájá Garha, Rájá * * *. The fighting men of this country are chiefly infantry, the horsemen being few. From the earliest establishment of the Muhammadan power in India no monarch had been able to reduce the fortresses of this country or to annex the territory.

At the time when Ásaf Khán received the *jágír* of Karra, and accomplished the conquest of Panna, the government of this country was in the hands of Rání Durgávatí, commonly known as "the Rání." She was highly renowned for her courage, ability, and liberality, and by the exercise of these qualities she had brought the whole country under her rule. The author has heard from intelligent men who have been there that she had twenty-three thousand inhabited villages under her sway. Twelve thousand of these were managed by her own *shikkdárs*, and the remainder were in the possession of tributary chiefs. The heads of the various clans paid their homage to her. She was the daughter of a Rájá of the tribe of Chandel, who was named Sálibáhan, who was Rájá of Ratah and Mahoba.[1] He married her to Dalpat, a son of Aman Dás. He did not belong to a high tribe, but he was wealthy, and as evil times had fallen upon Rájá Sálibáhan, he had consented to this alliance.

This Aman Dás rendered valuable assistance to Sultán Bahádur Gujarátí in the reduction of Ráísín; he had consequently been promoted, and had received the title of Sangrám Sháh. He was the son of Arjun Dás, son of Sukhan Dás, son of Gorak Dás, son of Kharjí. From old times there had been an ancestor in the house of the ruler of Garha holding a respectable position; but Kharjí, by his superior intelligence and tact, managed to acquire something in the way of tribute from the other chiefs of that country, and raised a force amounting to a hundred horse and ten thousand foot. His son, Sukhan Dás, carrying out the plans of his father, raised his army to five hundred horse and sixty thousand foot, enlisting many Rájpúts both in his cavalry

[1] See *suprà* Vol. IV. p. 462, note. The print and the MS. agree in the names as here given.

and infantry. He found two clever and able assistants, one belonging to the Kharchali tribe dwelling at Hamírpúr, and the other belonging to the tribe of Parihár.[1] Under him the government was carried on with great intelligence and vigour. His son Arjun succeeded him in the fortieth year (of his age). After him came Aman Dás, above mentioned.

This Aman Dás was an ill-disposed crafty fellow. He constantly opposed the will of his father, and engaged in evil pursuits. His father several times put him in confinement, and then endeavoured to bind him with covenants and promises. But the graceless fellow again relapsed into his evil courses, and having been guilty of some disgraceful actions, he fled to Rájá Nar Sing Deo, grandfather of Rájá Ram Chandar of Panna. Rájá Nar Sing treated him as a son, and when the Rájá went to attend upon Sultán Sikandar Lodí, he left him behind with his son Parbihan, who was then a minor. There he acted with great intelligence. His father, Arjun Dás, being dissatisfied with his ill-conducted son, appointed his son Jogí Dás to be his heir; but he, having regard to his elder brother's rights, did not accept this position.

Aman Dás, having heard of his father's intentions, made a rapid journey, and concealed himself in his mother's house. There, with the assistance of one of the Rájá's attendants, with whom he had long had relations, he one night killed his father. The men of the place then assembled and made him prisoner, and sent a person to communicate the facts to his brother. But the younger brother would not fall in with their views; he refused to do anything against his elder brother, who stood to him in the position of a father, and said that as his brother had chosen to risk eternal perdition, how could he look him in the face? All persuasion was useless, and he went off into the wilds.

The two confidential friends of the father were true to duty, and would not recognize his succession. They sent an account

[1] See Glossary, Index, "Parihar."

of the occurrence to Rájá Nar Singh Deo, and urged him to take possession of the territory. The Rájá took leave of Sultán Sikandar, and returned with a strong force. Aman Dás secured himself in the mountains; but as he could not hold out against the power of the Rájá, he opened communications, and said that as he had in his folly and wickedness killed one father, how could he then make war upon another? When the Rájá had overrun the territory, and left his officers in charge of it, Aman Dás came to meet him on his road, attended by only a few followers. After great display of weeping, the Rájá forgave him and restored his country. He kept up continual lamentation for his crime, and it is difficult to say whether this was mere hypocrisy, or whether the contrition he exhibited to his people was really sincere. When Aman Dás died, the succession devolved upon his son Dalpat, who ruled seven years and then died.

According to report Aman Dás, who received the name of Sangrám, had really no son. It is said that he induced Gobind Dás Kachhwáha, one of his attendants, to allow his wife, who was pregnant, to be delivered in his (Aman's) female apartments. If a daughter was born, it was to belong to the father; but if a boy, Aman Dás was to acknowledge it as his own, and no one should know anything about it. Gobind Dás acquiesced, and a boy was born, who was represented to be the Rájá's son. He received the name of Dalpat, and was married to Rání Durgávatí. When he died, he left a son, named BírNárayan, only five years of age. With the assistance of Adhár Káyath, the Rání assumed the government, showing no want of courage and ability, and managing her foreign relations with judgment and prudence. She carried on some great wars against Báz Bahádur and his officers, and was everywhere victorious. She had as many as twenty thousand excellent horse soldiers, and a thousand fine elephants. The treasures of the Rájás of that country came into her possession. She was a good shot, both with the bow and musket, and frequently went out hunting, when she used to bring down the animals with her own gun. When she heard of a tiger, she never rested till she had shot it. Many stories of her courage and daring are current in Hindústán. But she had one great fault. She listened to the voice of flatterers, and being puffed up with ideas of her power, she did not pay her allegiance to the Emperor.

When Ásaf Khán conquered the country of Panna, the Rání Durgávatí, infatuated with the ideas of her army, her courage, and her ability, took no heed of her new neighbour. Ásaf Khán at first kept up friendly and conciliatory relations with her; but he sent sharp spies and shrewd merchants into her country to get information of the communications and ways of ingress and egress. When he had obtained information of the wealth and treasures of this woman, he conceived the idea of making himself master of the country. He began first with ravaging the frontier villages, and went on until in the present year he received the Imperial command to effect the conquest of Garha.

Twelfth Year of the Reign.

Sulaimán Kiráni of Bengal.

[Text, vol. ii. p. 409.] While the Emperor was engaged in the siege of Chítor, Sulaimán Kiráni of Bengal again had the Emperor's name recited in the *khutba,* and made a wolf-like peace with Mun'im Khán Khán-khánán. The facts of the case are as follows:—When Mubáriz Khán, better known as 'Adalí, set up pretensions to royalty (in Bengal), Táj Khán Kiráni with his brothers fled to Bihár. There he pursued an artful and wily course, both in the days of Muhammad Khán, ruler of Bengal, who had rebelled, and afterwards also in the days of Bahádur Khán, until the time when 'Adalí was slain fighting against Bahádur Khán. When, after some time, the latter died, his brother Jalálu-d dín advanced his claim to the sovereignty of Bengal and Bihár. Táj Khán and his brothers were sometimes opposed to him, sometimes in league with him. He also made an artful and hypocritical friendship with Khán-zamán. When Jalálu-d dín died, Táj Khán obtained possession of Bengal and Bihár. He shortly afterwards died, and his younger brother Sulaimán succeeded, and established his authority over the two provinces. Sulaimán kept up a sort of friendship with Khán-zamán, and looking sharply after his own interests, he strengthened his position. Numbers of roving Afgháns gathered round him, and he amassed wealth and gathered together many elephants. After Khán-zamán had received the punishment due unto his deeds, the Emperor appointed Mun'im Khán Khán-khánán to the government of Jaunpúr. Asadu-lla Khán, an officer of Khán-zamán, had charge of Zamániya, a place built by Khán-zamán, and on the death of the Khán, Asadu-lla, in his stupidity, sent a person to Sulaimán, offering to surrender the place to him and to become his subject. But Mun'im Khán having got information of this, sent some persons to Asadu-lla, who induced him to forego this determination, and to repair in person to Khán-khánán. The Afghán army, which had come up with the intention of taking possession of Zamániya, went back disappointed. Lodí Afghán, who was the chief minister of Sulaimán, and remarkable for his wisdom and intelligence, was on the banks of the Sone. He knew Mun'im Khán Khán-khánán to be a man desirous of peace, so he entered into friendly relations with him, hoping thus to secure his own territories from the attacks of the Imperial forces. Presents and letters passed between them, strengthening their friendship. Meanwhile the Emperor was engaged in the siege of Chítor, and Sulaimán was occupied in subduing the Rájá of Orissa and Ibráhím.

But Sulaimán was ill at ease about Khán-khánán; so, while the Emperor was besieging Chítor, he sought to establish amity with him, Lodí being his medium. After some correspondence, it was arranged that Khán-khánán should pay Sulaimán a visit, to establish friendship between the Emperor and Sulaimán, and to arrange for the Emperor's name and titles being read in the *khutba* and impressed upon the coins. Khán-khánán determined to go and effect the objects in view, although many wise and sagacious persons endeavoured to dissuade him. But he paid no heed to them, and proceeded to Patna on his visit, attended by three hundred chosen men and by several of his officers and their attendants, numbering altogether about one thousand men. Lodí came to meet him, and show him proper respect. Then came Báyazíd, eldest son of Sulaimán; and at five *kos* from Patna, Sulaimán himself came forth to give him a formal state reception. Sulaimán conducted him to his own dwelling, and there gave him a sumptuous entertainment. The Imperial name was read out in the pulpit, coins were struck with it, and suitable tribute (to the Emperor) was presented. But a party of Sulaimán's turbulent adherents formed the design of seizing Khán-khánán, while the Emperor was engaged at Chítor with his great nobles, and while there was no one left at the capital who could interfere with their designs upon the Khán. When Lodí became acquainted with this conspiracy, he [*endeavoured to divert them from their purpose*]. Sulaimán assented to his views, but the fierce Afgháns would not listen to his words. Khán-khánán got information of the plot, and, with the advice of Lodí, he got away from his camp by a clever stratagem, and galloped off, attended by a small well-mounted escort. He was a long way off before the Afgháns were aware of his escape; and as they had failed in their purpose, they affected to maintain a friendly feeling. Báyazíd and Lodí hastened after the Khán, and, after showing him great honour and respect, they returned. Khán-khánán crossed the Ganges, and after two or three stages, he received the despatch of the conquest of Chítor.

Sulaimán now returned re-assured to Bengal, and devoted his attention to his own affairs. He treacherously seized upon the country of Orissa, in which the temple of Jagannáth is situated, and perfidiously killed the Rájá. Ibráhím [Sultán of Dehlí],[1] who was not quite right in his mind, and was soured by his fall from his lofty position, had taken refuge with the Rájá of Orissa,

[1] See *suprà*, Vol. V. p. 245.

and still dreamed of sovereignty. Sulaimán, by promises and oaths, got Ibráhím into his clutches, and then sent him to the next world.

Seventeenth Year of the Reign.

Battle of Sarnál.

(See Vol. V. p. 345.)

[1] Two hours before nightfall they fell in with a brahman, who informed them that the enemy with a large force had halted in the town of Sarnál, on the bank of the Sakánír, about four *kos* distant. On receiving this information, the Emperor held a council, and Jalál Khán urged that, as their own forces had not come up, and the enemy was in great strength, it was inexpedient to fight by day: they should either wait for reinforcements, or fall upon the enemy by night. But this sensible and prudent counsel did not please the Emperor, who said it was unworthy of brave warriors, and that it was advisable to make a dashing attack at once. "Let each one of us," said he, "single out his adversary and bring him down." * * * Trusting in heaven, they went on their course, till they came in sight of Sarnál. His Majesty went on a little in advance, to the bank of the Mahindarí,[2] to arrange his men. He gave orders for them to buckle on their armour; and when he thus prepared for the assault, he had not with him more than forty men.

Intelligence was now brought of the approach of the heads of his columns; but he was so angry at their tardiness, that he declared none of them should share in the honours of the fight. But he was informed that they had lost their way, and that Sháhbáz Khán, who had been sent to hasten their arrival, had been long in reaching them. This statement appeased his anger. Among the chiefs of the army who now came up and joined him were Khán-i 'Álam, Saiyid Mahmúd

[1] The text of this and the two following Extracts is wanting in the Lucknow edition.

[2] The Mahindarí is the Mahí (see Vol. V. p. 435.)

Khán Bárha, Rájá Bhagwant Dás, Sháh Kulí Khán Mahram, Kúnwar Mán Singh, Bábá Khán Kakshál, Bhúpat, Salím Khán Kákar, Bhúj Hájí, Yúsuf Khán, and some others. The whole force now amounted to about 200 men. As they were crossing the river, Mán Singh requested that he might be appointed to the advanced force. His Majesty said that he had no army to divide, but on that day they must all fight heartily together. But Mán Singh earnestly entreated that, in order to show his devotion, he might be allowed to push on a few paces in front. He received permission, and with a few brave men went on in advance. Akbar himself and his companions followed, and all passed over the river safely at a ford.

Ibráhím Husain Mirzá had previously entered the town of Sarnál. When he saw the dust of the approaching force, and the way in which the horsemen crossed the river, he told his companions that he was sure that the Emperor was there present. But the ill-starred foolish man led his forces out of the town to a rising ground, and there took up a position. When the Emperor's men had come out of the river, they were scattered and broken up into parties, each of which pushed on as best it could. The Emperor himself, with a few followers, approached the river-gate of Sarnál, where he was encountered by a party of the rebels. But Mukbil Khán, a Kalmuck slave, rushed forward with a few brave fellows, and soon watered the dust with their blood. On entering the town, they found it full of men, and learned that Ibráhím Husain Mirzá had gone out by another way to prepare for battle.

The Emperor, having disentangled himself from the streets of the town, and the crowds of people, endeavoured to encourage his followers, and to strike dismay into the enemy. Bábá Khán Kákshál, with a party of brave men, assaulted, and bore back the enemy. Others also, as they got clear from the streets of the town, came up in all directions, and took part in the fight. Among them Bhúpat, the brother of Rájá Bhagwant Dás, met his death bravely fighting with a party of the enemy he had encountered. The ground was rugged, and so covered with thorn hedges, that two horsemen could not proceed abreast. His Majesty still pressed on slowly, and was supported by Rájá Bhagwant Dás. Three of the enemy now attacked them. One menaced Bhagwant Dás with his javelin; but the Rájá stood up in his stirrups, and avoiding the weapon, he struck his adversary so fiercely with his spear that he was glad to retreat. The other two attacked the Emperor, and a formidable hedge prevented Khán-i 'Álam and others from rendering any assistance; but the Emperor dashed from the hedge upon his adversaries so fiercely that they turned and fled. Ibráhím Husain, who was fighting manfully, finding himself defeated, turned and fled. The royal troops pursued and cut down many of the fugitives.

Affairs of Bengal.

(See Vol. V. pp. 372, 511.)

When the death of Sulaimán Kiráni became known, Khán-khánán Mun'im Khán marched from the fort of Chunár against the province of Bihár. Sikandar Uzkek died about the same time. Khán-khánán then sent Tangri Kulí with a force against Hájípúr, and Tálibí with another detachment against Patna. Gújar, unable to resist, sent presents and propositions of submission. He offered to enter the Imperial service, and to assist in the conquest of Bengal, upon condition of receiving Gorakpúr for the support of himself and family, and of the province of Bihár being allotted in *jágír* to the Imperial nobles; or that the *sarkár* of Hájípúr and Bihár should be assigned to him for that year, he being responsible to the Imperial treasury for the revenue, and that in the next year he should receive a *jágír* in Bengal. Mun'im Khán accepted this proposition, and was about to make Gorakpúr over to him, when Lodí, whose craft appeared in all the matters of that country, conspired with Háshim Khán, and upset the arrangement. Gújar, finding that he had nothing to expect from Mun'im Khán, was obliged to side with Lodí.

Mun'im Khán, having received tribute from Lodí, started on his return, when intelligence arrived that Yúsuf Muhammad had taken possession of Gorakpúr. Mun'im Khán had taken this Yúsuf Muhammad, son of Sulaimán Uzbek, to Court, and had brought his misconduct to the notice of the Emperor, who deemed it prudent to put him in confinement. But when His Majesty went on his campaign in Gujarát, Yúsuf escaped from his prison in Ágra, and wrested Gorakpúr from the hands of the men of Páyinda Muhammad Bangash. When Mun'im Khán was informed of this, he immediately ordered Khán Muhammad Basúdí and Páyinda Muhammad Bangash to repress the revolt. He himself also marched from the town of Muhammadábád along with Muhammad Kulí Khán Birlás, Majnún Khán Kákshál, and some other nobles. But on the march Majnún Khán, with all the Káksháls, parted from him. The reason of this defection was, that false statements had been made to Majnún Khán, that Bábá Khán Jabbárí, Mirzá Muhammad Sháh, and the other Káksháls who had accompanied the Emperor on the campaign in Gujarát, had killed Sháhbáz Khán, and had gone over to join the Mirzás. In consequence of this, it was asserted that an order had arrived for the arrest of Majnún Khán. The Khán-khánán sent officers to re-assure Majnún Khán, and to bring him with them. But their efforts were in vain, until letters arrived from Bábá Khán detailing the favours received from His Majesty, and the services he had rendered in the campaign. Ashamed of his suspicions, Majnún Khán returned and rejoined the army of Khán-khánán; but before he arrived, Khán-khánán had accomplished the reduction of Gorakpúr.

Meanwhile Dáúd, puffed up with pride, had marched against Jaunpúr, having sent on Lodí in advance with a select force and the elephants. He obtained possession of Zamániya by the capitulation of Muhammad Kásim, the *muhr-dár* (seal-bearer). Khán-khánán collected the *amirs* under his command, and sent forward a strong force against Dáúd, he himself following more leisurely. * * Lodí was greatly elated with the capture of Zamániya, and he sent 5000 or 6000 men across the Ganges, under the command of Yúsuf Muhammad, who had escaped from Gorakpúr and joined the Afghâns. After he had crossed the Ganges, Mirzá Husain Khán and Rájá Gajpati attacked and defeated him, inflicting heavy loss. Muhammad Kulí Khán Birlás and other *amirs* joined the victors, with considerable reinforcements, at Gházípúr. Khán-khánán also arrived with a strong force. Lodí threw up fortifications between the rivers Sáh (Sye) and Ganges, and there held his ground. Combats took place every day between the bold spirits of the two armies. But although the Imperial forces maintained a bold attitude, they were inferior in men, elephants, and guns. The Emperor was at the time engaged in the siege of Surat: so Mun'im Khán offered terms of peace; but Lodí haughtily rejected them. The *amirs* in the royal army were in a depressed condition, and were neither inclined to fight nor retire. But the Imperial good fortune attended them, and Lodí accepted terms of peace and withdrew.

The reason of this was, that when Dáúd came to Mongír from Bengal, he made away with Yúsuf, the son of Táj, and nephew to himself, in the apprehension that Lodí might support him. Lodí had been an old servant of Táj, and he had given his own daughter in marriage to Yúsuf; but his intercessions for him were of no avail. When Lodí became acquainted with the fact, he deserted Dáúd, and joined Mun'im Khán, sending suitable tribute to the Emperor. Dáúd, on ascertaining this defection, fell back, and shut himself up in the fort of Garhí, where he scattered the treasure of his father among his soldiers. Jalál Khán, Saiyid Húrí, and Kálá Pahár, whose name was Rájú, now separated from Lodí, and divisions arose in Lodí's forces. Lodí was thereby compelled to abandon his design of attacking Dáúd, and to take refuge in the fort of Rohtás. He wrote from thence to assure Mun'im Khán of his fidelity to the

Emperor, and calling for his support. The Khán sent him aid, and looked anxiously for the return of the Emperor.

Christians at Surat.

(See Vol. V. p. 351.)

Whilst the siege of Surat was proceeding, a large party of Christians from the port of Goa arrived, and they were admitted to an audience of the Emperor, although it is probable that they had come to assist the besieged, and to get the fort into their own hands. But when they saw the strength of the Imperial force, and its power of carrying on the siege, they represented themselves to be ambassadors, and besought the honour of an interview. They offered various articles of the country as presents. Akbar treated each one them with great condescension, and conversed with them about the affairs of Portugal, and other European matters.

Eighteenth Year of the Reign.

I'dar and Dúngarpúr.

(See Vol. V. p. 353.)

[Text, vol. iii. p. 8.] [When the Emperor set out from Gujarát on his return to A'gra], he appointed Muzaffar Khán to the government of Málwa. He also sent Mán Singh, Sháh Kulí Khán Mahram, and * * * * and a strong force, to proceed by I'dar to Dúngarpúr and that neighbourhood, to reduce to subjection the *zamíndárs,* and afterwards to proceed to A'gra. * * * * The Emperor reached the capital on the 2nd Safar, 981, and soon afterwards Mán Singh, and the other *amírs* who had gone by way of I'dar, rejoined the Imperial standard. When this chief and his followers reached Dúngarpúr, they found the *zamíndárs* of that country prepared to resist. Mán Singh defeated them, and inflicted great loss upon them. After ravaging the country, he went, in accordance with orders, to U'dípúr, the country of theRáná. TheRáná came forth to meet him, and received with proper submission the royal robe which had been sent to him. He conducted Mán Singh to his own abode, and there entertained him. Some treacherous designs entered the mind of the Ráná, but he was dissuaded from them by his well-wishers, and Mán Singh went his way in peace.

Muzaffar Khán.

(See Vol. V. p. 370.)

[Text, vol. iii. p. 8.] Muzaffar Khán arrived to attend upon His Majesty, and was raised to the dignity of minister. An order had been sent from Gujarát, directing him to quit the place he might be in, and to repair at once to the Royal presence. He accordingly hastened from Sárangpúr to the capital, and then was installed in office. * * * * But in a short time he became proud, conceited, and self-willed, so that he looked upon his position as due to his own merit, not to the favour of the Emperor. After a time, when the matter of the *dágh* (horse-branding) came under consideration, he was too puffed up in his own conceit to inquire into the matter, but talked foolishly about it. * * * * [When the Emperor was about to embark on his campaign against Patna], he offered the command of the camp of the Imperial household to Muzaffar Khán; but he further increased the displeasure of the Emperor by making improper objections to his acceptance of this duty.

Nineteenth Year of the Reign.

Capture of Hájípúr.

(See Vol. V. p. 377.)

[Text, vol. iii. p. 75.] Khán-i 'Álam procured a number of experienced pilots, and embarking in boats on the evening of the 24th Amurdád, the pilots conducted the force across the river so cleverly that the enemy knew nothing of it. Then they ascended the small stream which parts from the Ganges and flows past Hájípúr. The enemy, greatly astonished at the sight, opened a furious fire of cannon and musketry, and the assailants were on the point of being defeated. A number of *ghrábs* which the Emperor had near him were now sent to their support. The enemy endeavoured to stop them, but they were unable to make way against the stream, and failed in the attempt. The royal boats then proceeded to Hájípúr by the river Gandak. They were met with a very heavy fire, but could not be stopped, and disembarking they made an assault upon the place. It was captured after some severe fighting. Some rascals set the town on fire, and began to plunder; but the forts were taken possession of by the royal forces.

Garhí and Tánda.

(See Vol. V. p. 381.)

[Text, vol. iii. p. 84.] Garhí is the gate of Bengal. On one side of it is a lofty mountain, very difficult of ascent, even for a man on foot, how then can a horseman get up it? On the other side several rivers join the Ganges. In the midst a strong fortress had been built by the rulers of the country. A council of war was held as to the way of attacking it, and it was resolved that some way of access must be sought. The *zamíndárs* of the neighbourhood said that there was a secret way through the country of the Teli Rájá, which, though impracticable for beasts of burden, might be surmounted by active and intelligent horsemen. * * * Majnún Khán was sent at the head of a brave and resolute detachment by this route. Kiyá Khán Gang was directed to proceed towards Garhí with a party of friendly *zamíndárs*. The rest of the army was about to march, when the sight of the Imperial forces completely overawed the enemy. The leading forces of Khán-khánán made them waver; but when Kiyá Khán's force appeared, they were filled with consternation, and took to flight. A place thus strong, by the help of God, fell without a struggle! * * *

On the 23rd Mihr the Emperor reached Iskandarpúr, near to Manikpúr, where he received a despatch from Khán-khánán, announcing that Dáúd had fled, and that the Imperial troops had occupied Tánda, the capital. When Garhí fell, Dáúd, unable to contend against the victorious forces, had retreated before them. At Tánda the river Ganges separates into two branches. One flows towards Sátgánw and Orissa; the other towards Mahmúdábád, Fathábád, Sunargánw, and Chittagánw. Dáúd followed the course of the river of Sátgánw until he reached the confines of Orissa, in the hope of continuing his resistance there. Khán-khánán then entered and occupied Tánda, which is the central point of Bengal.

Twentieth Year of the Reign.

Revolt in Bengal.

(See Vol. V. p. 390.)

[Text, vol. iii. p. 109.] Whilst Khán-khánán was absent on the campaign against Dáúd in Katak, Kálá Pahár, Babúí Mangalí, and a number of disaffected Afgháns, took arms and attacked the Káksháls. These made but a faint resistance, and were dishonoured by their pusillanimity. The Afgháns occupied the territory of Ghorá-ghát, and pursued the Káksháls, not allowing them to draw rein until they reached Tánda. The Khán-khánán returned in haste, and, without entering Tánda, proceeded at once against the enemy. He found the turbulent force posted on the other side of the Ganges. Not far off the river divides into two branches. Over one of these he cast a bridge, and was preparing to do so over the other, when the enemy took the alarm and fled. Khán-khánán then proceeded to Málda, and sent a detachment under Majnún Khán to Ghorá-ghát, which quickly brought the place again under the Imperial authority.

Warlike operations in Bihár.

(See Vol. V. p. 380.)

[Text, vol. iii. p. 109.] It has been already stated that when Akbar returned from the conquest of Patna, he deemed it expedient to send Muzaffar Khán to serve as an assistant to Farhat Khán in the siege of Rohtás, without allowing him the honour of an interview. The Khán was for some time stunned with his disgrace; but he at length listened to the prudent counsels of Khwája Shamsu-d dín Kháfí, and bringing out some of his hoards, he busied himself in equipping his forces. He soon obtained possession of Júndh and Sahsarám, which, in consequence of the Emperor's having been so fully occupied, had not been assigned in *jágír* to any one. He trained and prepared his forces carefully, and when Farhat Khán, with the other *amírs*, invested Rohtás, he showed himself fully ready for service, and soon proved his valour. Bahádur, the son of Haibat Khán, made a sortie from the fortress. He was opposed by Muzaffar Khán, who drove him back with a considerable loss of munitions and elephants. The *amírs* proceeded to invest the fortress, and he, attaching himself to Farhat Khán, exhibited great diligence.

In a short time, the conduct of Muzaffar Khán won back the Royal favour. The Emperor addressed a letter to him, with instructions to prosecute the siege of Rohtás if he and the *amírs* with him considered that the place might be reduced in a given time; but if the opinion was that the siege would be protracted, he was to raise it and employ his forces against the Afgháns, who were creating disturbances in Bihár, and to compel them to become dutiful subjects of the Imperial throne, or else to inflict condign punishment upon them. Muzaffar Khán replied that the army was not possessed of the implements for carrying on a siege, and that the probable time of its fall could not be calculated,—it therefore seemed desirable to first rid the province of the contemptible enemy who distressed it. He accordingly joined Mírzáda 'Alí Khán and the other warriors who had been left in the province by the Emperor. He also formed a union with Muhsin Khán, 'Arab Bahádur, and the forces which had been left under them by Mun'im Khán to protect his *jágír*. With these he rendered good service, and repressed all the malcontents in the province. He drove Adham

Khán Mutanabbi out of Ibráhímpúr, and Daryá Khán from the town of Jasarkánur to Jhárkand.

When he had thus restored order, the officers of Mun'im Khán were moved with envy against him, and sent him away. As he had no *jágír* on which to support his followers, he retired with Khudádád Birlás and Khwája Shamsu-d dín to Júndh and Sahsarám. As he was on his way thither, intelligence reached him that those two places had been occupied by forces from Rohtás. So he continued his march, and by valour and good management cleared those two places of the enemy. He had no sooner done this than new disturbances broke out in Bihár. Disregarding the ungrateful behaviour of the Bihár officials, he once more intervened, and rendered good service.

The circumstances of the case were these. Mun'im Khan Khán-khánán had left 'Arab Bahádur in Mahír, which is a fort between Bihár and Jhárkand. Ghází and Hájí, two brothers, came with a party of turbulent Afgháns from Jhárkand, and seized the place. Many of the garrison were put to the sword; but 'Arab Bahádur made his escape, and, hastening to the *amírs* of the province, they gathered their forces, and marched to repress this outbreak. The Afgháns retired to the fastnesses of the mountains and defied them. The *amírs* went after them, and at length found themselves unable either to advance or retire. A party of nearly 300 Rájpúts, in the service of Rájá Bhagwant Dás, bravely advanced, but were defeated, and lost nearly 100 of their number. They now sent to solicit aid from Muzaffar Khán, who soon joined them with his victorious followers.

A letter at this time arrived from Khán-khánán, which made them hesitate in their movements. It brought the information that Junaid was hastening by way of Jhárkand to Bihár, and urged the necessity of overpowering him before he could obtain reinforcements. Muzaffar Khán took a bold view of the matter, and resolved that the proper course was to crush the rebel Afgháns before Junaid could join them. There was no knowing whether Junaid would reach the neighbourhood in less than ten days, and it was to be hoped that the enemy before them might be routed in one day, after which the Imperial forces would be in a better condition to meet the intruder. It was accordingly determined that a detachment should proceed with all speed and caution, and get close in to the rear of the enemy, while the main force prepared for battle in front. Muzaffar Khán commanded the centre, Farhat Khán the right, and * * * Khwája Shamsu-d dín was placed in command of the force which was to gain the enemy's rear.

The enemy was posted on a hill, full of confidence in their numbers, and in the strength of their position. When they found themselves suddenly threatened both in front and rear, they were seized with dismay and fled. The Imperial troops achieved a victory, and secured much spoil. They followed in pursuit until they reached a hill near Rámpúr, in Jhárkand, where the enemy made a stand. * * Muzaffar Khán made his dispositions in front, and Khwája Shamsu-d dín, as before, got to the rear of the enemy, and attacked bravely. Husain Khán and * * several leaders of the enemy having fallen, the rebels fled, and the Imperial troops gained a decisive victory. After returning thanks for their success, they withdrew, and repaired to their respective cantonments.

The news of this victory arrested Junaid for a time in his contemplated attack upon Bihár. But a few days afterwards he found the means of reaching Nuzhatábád in that province, and there raised a revolt. The *amirs* of the province withdrew into Patna, and in their distress again applied to Muzaffar Khán for help. He accordingly moved to their assistance. On his march, he was met by letters from the Emperor, acknowledging and eulogizing his services, and conferring upon him the *jágír* of Hájípúr previously held by Muhammad Kulí Khán Birlás. This stimulated him to further exertions. He effected a junction with the other *amirs*, and began operations against the insurgents. He erected a bridge by which he passed over the Punpun river.

But instructions now arrived from Khán-khánán, directing caution in attacking Junaid, as he himself intended to march against him. The *amírs* concurred in this policy of procrastination, and although Muzaffar Khán advised a bolder course, his counsels were of no avail. He was adverse to remaining quiet or retreating, and was about to attack Junaid, when great alarm was raised by disturbances which had broken out at Hájípúr, and he was obliged to repair thither.

Táj Khán Panwár and others had attacked Mír Mahmúd Shaukiti, who held Hájípúr for Muzaffar Khán, and had killed him and about a hundred of his people. So Muzaffar Khán was constrained to relinquish his designs against Junaid, and he proceeded with Khudádád Birlás and others to Hájípúr. Notwithstanding the numbers of his opponents, he determined to attack them. As a direct advance against them was impracticable, he crossed the Ganges, and came to the town of Sawánih, between which place and Hájípúr the river Gandak runs with a strong current. The Afgháns were confident in their numbers, and in the weakness of their foes. But Muzaffar had resolution, which is the key of success and of victory. He was joined by Udí Karan, the *zamíndár* of Champáran.

While the enemy was on one side of the river, and Muzaffar was on the other, seeking some way of getting over, the *zamíndár* suggested a way of accomplishing this difficult operation. He said that higher up the river his people had some strong boats, in which the troops might be conveyed over. * * Three hundred men under Kásim 'Alí Sístání, etc., were sent over the river by night, attended by messengers, who were to bring intelligence of the passage having been safely effected. When the information was brought that this detachment had crossed over and were approaching the enemy, Muzaffar Khán sent some boats full of men over the river, under the command of Khwája Shamsu-d dín and Khudádád Birlás, to attack the enemy in front. The Afgháns received them with the fire of matchlocks, and showers of arrows; but in the midst of the fight, the drums of the force which had been sent to their rear spread a panic among the Afgháns, and they took flight. Many of them were slain. Hájípúr was delivered from them, and great spoil fell into the hands of the victors. The inhabitants of Patna had watched the proceedings with malicious interest, but refrained from rendering the rebels any assistance, though they were filled with disappointment.

After achieving this success, Muzaffar Khán received information that Fath Khán Musazai, and some others, had assembled a large force of Afgháns on the other side of the river Gandak, with the intention of raising disturbances. Muzaffar Khán, in his foresight and zeal, set forth at once to oppose them. On reaching the river, he went with a party to reconnoitre, and endeavour to find a place to cross over; for although the river is narrow, it is very deep. While thus engaged, he saw a party of the enemy's horse, about 200 in number He immediately gave directions to Khwája Shamsu-d dín and 'Arab Bahádur to make a detour, cross over the river, and attack them unawares. They obeyed; but the enemy, perceiving their approach, fell back to obtain assistance. Muzaffar Khán then passed over the river, to join his advanced force. The flying enemy, being joined by reinforcements, faced round and gave battle. The great numbers of the enemy struck terror into the Imperialists, so that they dispersed and fled. Many threw themselves into the river, and were drowned. Muzaffar Khán was about to plunge into the river, when Khwája Shamsu-d dín seized his bridle, and made off towards the mountains; but he sent back a swift horseman to the camp, to try and bring up more men. The enemy pressed on in pursuit, but Khwája Shamsu-d dín, 'Arab Bahádur, and others, about fifty in all, turned round and checked their advance with showers of arrows. Night was coming on, and Muzaffar Khán was in this strait, when the blaze of the Imperial good fortune shone forth.

A report had reached the camp of Muzaffar Khán that he had been killed, and the men were about to hasten off, when the messenger who had been sent back arrived and revived their drooping spirits. Khudádád Birlás, Mihr 'Alí, and about 200 men boldly dashed across the river, and the messenger who had been sent for them took back the intelligence of their approach. The enemy, notwithstanding their success and the excess of their numbers, were unable to stand against the assault of this gallant band, but took to flight. Defeat was thus turned into victory, and great booty was won. Next day they plundered the camp of the Afgháns, and obtained much spoil. The machinations of the enemy were thus defeated. Those who escaped went and sought refuge with Táj Khán Panwár. There they pursued their evil designs, and in the abundance of their wealth, the paucity of their wisdom, and the numbers of adventurers, they again took the offensive.

Muzaffar Khán prudently effected his retreat across the Gandak, and took up a position in a spot bounded on three sides by the river, and on the fourth by a great swamp. There he busied himself in collecting men and stores. The enemy, emboldened by this retreat, came up and surrounded the force of Muzaffar Khán; but being unable to make any impression upon it, they were disheartened. In the course of a few days Muzaffar's men increased in numbers and recovered their spirits. The *zamíndárs* of the neighbourhood also took heart, and exerted themselves in furnishing things required. A bridge was then thrown over the river. To obviate any disaster in crossing, it was prudently resolved to send over by night a party of men, who were to make an entrenchment as a defence against the enemy, so that the troops might be able to deploy when they should get to the other side. But no one was willing to undertake this duty till Khwája Shamsu-d dín Kháfí boldly volunteered for the perilous work. He soon crossed over, and the Afgháns retreated before him, in the expectation that the Imperial troops, finding their opponents in retreat, would disperse in search of plunder, and afford a favourable opportunity for attacking them. Muzaffar Khán took all proper precautions, and sent a strong force over to make the place secure. The Afgháns, aware of the movement, threw off all concealment, and moved a strong division against this advanced force. The infantry gave way, and their flight caused a panic among a body of horse. Their backward rush broke down the bridge, and near 300 men, horse and foot, perished in the river. Khwája Shamsu-d dín, Khudádád Birlás, and several other distinguished soldiers made a stand, and twice checked the advance of the enemy with showers of arrows. A third attack was made, but an arrow pierced the horse of Husain Khán, the commander of the enemy, and brought him down. The enemy then broke, and desisted from their attacks. No harm befel the brave Imperial soldiers. By dint of great exertion the bridge was repaired, and all the army passed over. The Afgháns then retired, and joined their main army under Táj Khán.

Muzaffar Khán followed them, and was informed by his scouts that a party of the rebels, in perfect ignorance of his approach, was seeking for a suitable position for earthworks. Muzaffar Khán left Khudádád in command of a small force, to secure his camp, and marched with the design of making the enemy's men prisoners. He fell suddenly upon them, and, after a short resistance, they fled precipitately. Many were killed, among whom was Táj Khán Panwár, whose head had been cut off and brought in by Hájí Pahlawán, without his knowing who the victim was. Jalál Khán Ghazní, one of their bravest chiefs, was taken prisoner, and many others were taken or slain. A complete victory was gained; but although nightfall and the thick growing trees prevented the destruction of the rebels' houses, many of the brave soldiers secured a good booty. Next morning the army advanced; but the enemy dispersed, and threw themselves into the river. Great numbers perished, but about 100 of the boldest succeeded in reaching the opposite shore. This revolt was thus entirely suppressed.

Soon after this, Satrí and Jatrí,[1] with a party of Afgháns,

[1] Names of two Afgháns.

seized the opportunity to take possession of the country of Bakra. This is a populous district, thirty *kos* long and twenty *kos* broad, in the vicinity of Mongír, by the river Ganges. When Muzaffar Khán was informed of this outbreak, he marched to suppress it. A sharp action followed, in which Fath Khán, the commander of the insurgents, and seventy-nine of his men, fell. Muzaffar then occupied the country.

These successes of Muzaffar Khán made Mun'im Khán Khán-khánán averse to his remaining in that neighbourhood, so he sent an order directing him to repair immediately to Court. * * * * But while Muzaffar was chafing in vexation, a command arrived from the Emperor, ordering him to remain where he was, and carry on his work until recalled by an Imperial order. So he returned joyfully to Hájípúr, * * * and shortly afterwards the far-seeing Emperor, appreciating his services and merits, bestowed upon him the wide territory extending from the ford of Chaunsá to Garhí.

Rájá Todar Mal.

[Text, vol. iii. p. 138.] Rájá Todar Mal now arrived at Court, bringing with him fifty-four elephants, which had been taken in Bengal, in the campaign of Takrohi. These he presented, and he made a report upon the state of the country. He received many marks of favour, and was promoted to the dignity of *díwán*, and to the charge of the revenue and civil affairs of the Empire. He was an honest sincere man, and devoid of avarice. Would that he had been free from hatred and revenge, and that harshness had not been so conspicuous in his character!

Twenty-first Year of the Reign.

Conquest of Siwána.

[Text, vol. iii. p. 147.] Siwána is a famous fortress in the province of Ajmír, and belonged to Chandar Sen.[1] It was held by Bathá Ráhtor. Sháh Kulí Khán Mahram and Rái

[1] "Son of Mál Deo."—Faizí Sirhindí.

Singh had not conducted their operations skilfully. The horses of their men were out of condition, and want of grain and provender had reduced their army to a miserable state. Saiyid Ahmad and others were first sent to assist, and to do their best in reducing the fort, so that the troops might return. The *amirs* hastened from their estates to take their part in the siege. Just at this time Jalál Khán was killed, and this encouraged the rebels to raise their heads still higher in rebellion. More especially Kalla, son of Rái Rám, and grandson of Mál Deo, who collected a large number of men in the fort of Wíkúr. The Saiyids of Bárha and other chiefs of the army were directed to put down these rebels, and the operations against Siwána were suspended. Sháhbáz Khán was appointed to conduct a reinforcement, and return to Court. When he approached the scene of operations, he learned that the Imperial army had already invested the fortress, and were pressing it hard. Sháhbáz Khán pressed forward zealously, to take part in the siege. By vigorous and valiant exertions, the place was reduced, and the garrison made prisoners. Leaving a detachment under the Bárha Saiyids as a garrison, he marched against Siwána.

Eight *kos* from the fortress of Siwána, he came to a stone fort called Dúnára.[1] He found it occupied by a body of Rájpúts, of the Ráhtor clan, who refused his summons to surrender. So he set about the siege in earnest, and prepared *sábáts.* In a short time the fort was taken, and many of the Ráhtors were slain. He then marched against Siwána, the garrison of which place had been intimidated by the fall of Dúnára. He again constructed *sábáts*, and pressed on the operations of the siege so vigorously and boldly that the garrison, after a short delay, capitulated.

Death of Dáúd.

(See Vol. V. p. 400.)

[Text, vol. iii. p. 158.] When victory declared for the Imperial army, the weak-minded Dáúd was made prisoner. His horse

[1] On the Loní, thirty-five miles from Siwána.

stuck fast in the mud, and * * * a party of brave men seized him, and brought him prisoner to Khán-jahán. The Khán said to him, "Where is the treaty you made, and the oath that you swore?" Throwing aside all shame, he said, "I made that treaty with Khán-khánán. If you will alight, we will have a little friendly talk together, and enter into another treaty." Khán-jahán, fully aware of the craft and perfidy of the traitor, ordered that his body should be immediately relieved from the weight of his rebellious head. He was accordingly decapitated, and his head was sent off express to the Emperor. His body was exposed on a gibbet at Tánda, the capital of that country.

Campaign against Gajpati. Capture of Rohtás.

[Text, vol. iii. p. 161.] In consequence of the difficulty of transporting camp equipage, Gajpati[1] had broken out into rebellion, and formed the design of plundering Gházípúr. But Sháhbáz Khán arrived with the royal forces, and shook the foundations of his position. He fled to the ford of Chaunsá, pursued by the Imperial troops. There he crossed the Ganges, and continued fighting. The royal forces, having found means of crossing the river, pursued him, and inflicted upon him a severe defeat, taking his boats, guns, and camp equipage. In their pursuit of him, they came to the fort of Mahawá,[2] which they invested, and Sangrám, the commandant, immediately surrendered. Sháhbáz placed a garrison in it, and continued his pursuit of the rebel, who fled into the wooded and rugged country of Bhojpúr. All efforts to overtake him proving vain, the royal troops retired. On the following day the rebel attacked the retreating forces on the bank of a river, and kept up the fight till night. The ground was so broken and confined, that the royal troops were unable to cross in face of their assailants; but, being guided by Sangrám, they fell upon the baggage of the enemy. Unable to accomplish anything by day, the rebel

[1] Briggs calls him "Raja of Gunjowty."—Firishta, ii. p. 250.

[2] Twenty-eight miles north-west of Rohtás.

made a night attack, but being again defeated, he fled to Jagdespúr, one of his strongest retreats. For two months the royal forces were actively engaged in clearing away the trees round the fort. At length the place fell, and the family and property of the rebel was captured, but he himself escaped.

After this defeat, Gajpati fled in great distress and terror to the foot of the hills of Rohtás, and there concealed himself. Bari Sál, his brother, with a large body of rebels, sought refuge among the woods and defiles, but they were discovered and slain by the Imperial forces, and great spoil was captured.

When Gajpati was [first] defeated, he placed his son Sri Rám, with a body of rebels and the necessary armament, in the fort of Sher-garh.[1] Sháhbáz Khán invested this fort, constructed *sábáts*, and made regular approaches. The people of the neighbourhood were coming in and submitting to the Imperial government, when a great and unexpected piece of fortune fell upon him. At the time when this country had no (Imperial) noble to manage it, the fort of Rohtás fell into the hands of Junaid, and he placed it under the charge of Saiyid Muhammad, one of his most trusty adherents. On the death of Junaid, the Saiyid held the fort for some time as a rebel against the Imperial authority; but he at length induced his men to agree in sending tribute to the Emperor by the hands of some faithful adherent. When the Imperial army approached the fortress under the direction of guides, without whose help the access would have been difficult, they resolved to make submission, and capitulated. Muzaffar Khán also was approaching with the army of Bihár to attack the fortress. The garrison sent out officers to treat with Sháhbáz Khán and surrender the fort. He joyfully agreed to their terms, and took possession of the fortress. Upon hearing of the capitulation, Muzaffar Khán returned disappointed.

The fortress having thus fallen, the people of the hills were filled with alarm. Sri Rám surrendered the keys of Sher-garh to Sháhbáz Khán.

[1] Or "Shergutty," sixty-five miles S.E. of Jagdespúr.

TWENTY-SECOND YEAR OF THE REIGN.

The Mint.

[Text, vol. iii. p. 195.] On the 2nd Ázar, Muzaffar Khán, Rájá Todar Mal, and Khwája Sháh Mansúr were summoned to a council at Kot-pakalí, where many important matters were discussed and settled. Bihár was given to Shujá'at Khán, Mír Mu'izzu-l Mulk and other adherents. The mint of the Empire, which had been under the management of a *chaudhari*, was now divided.[1] That of Fathpúr was placed under the direction of Khwája 'Abdu-s Samad, the elegant penman (*shírín-kalam*); that of Lahore under Muzaffar Khán; of Bengal, under Rájá Todar Mal; of Jaunpúr, under Khwája Sháh Mansúr; of Gujarát, under Khwája 'Imádu-d dín Husain; and of Patna, under Ásaf Khán. On the same day an order was issued, directing the coinage of four-cornered rupees.

European Novelties.

[Text, vol. iii. p. 196.] Hájí Habíb had been sent to the port of Goa, with a large sum of money and intelligent artisans, to examine and bring to the Emperor's knowledge the various productions of art and skill to be found in that town. He now returned to Court, having with him a number of men clad in Christian garb, and beating drums and playing European instruments. He presented fabrics which he had selected. The artisans who had gone there to acquire knowledge exhibited their skill, and received applause. Musicians of that country played upon various instruments, especially upon the organ, and gave great delight to all who heard them.

Defeat of the Rájá of Madhgarh.

[Text, vol. iii. p. 196.] This *zamíndár* having been guilty of some overt acts, Sádik Khán was sent with a considerable force to induce him by kind words to return to his allegiance, or to

[1] The printed text has "*tafhím*," instead of the right word, "*taksím;*"—an absurd blunder, but not worse than many others.

compel him, if necessary. The Imperial force prepared to make its way through the jungle to the town of U'ndacha,[1] which is the principal place of that chief. When they approached the fort of Karhará,[2] they found that Paramánand Panwár had shut the fort, and prepared against a siege. The royal forces invested the place, and in short time it was compelled to capitulate. The army then pursued its march, but was greatly impeded by the dense woods. Cutting their way through, they reached the Satdhára,[3] on the north of U'ndacha. The army of the insurgent was arrayed for battle on its banks. Skirmishes went on for a day or two, and the Imperial army was at last directed to cross the river. [*Severe fighting, with varying results.*] The enemy were at length defeated and put to flight, and their camp was plundered. * * Horal Deo, the eldest son of the Rájá, was killed. * * Rám Sáh, another son, was wounded, and fled, and near 200 Rájpúts were slain.

Twenty-third Year of the Reign.

Conquest of Kombalmír.

(See Vol. V. p. 410.)

[Text, vol. iii. p. 205.] Kombalmír is a fortress situated upon a high mountain, and difficult of access. It was held by dependents of the *rána*, and few had been able to make any impression upon it in former times. * * * Sháhbáz Khán was sent in command of an army against this fortress. Rájá Bhagwant Dás, Kunwar Mán Singh, and other chiefs were directed to accompany him. * * On the 4th Farwardín, Sháhbáz invested the place. Fear and distraction fell upon the enemy, and by accident a large gun that was in the fort burst, and destroyed the magazine. The assailants immediately dashed up the hill. They encountered a large body of Rájpúts posted at a gate near the temple, who made a firm stand, but were cut to pieces, and the fort was

[1] Urcha on the Betwá, in Bundelkhand. It is the chief seat of the Bundelas.
[2] About eighteen miles south of Narwar.
[3] "Seven streams." The Betwá is so called at Urcha.

secured. The Ráná then fled to the hills of Bánswárra. Sháhbáz Khán placed Ghází Khán Badakhshi in command of the fort, and went in pursuit. The fort of Kokanda fell into his power, and he also captured the fort of U'dípúr, where he secured an immense booty.

Tribute of Bengal. Arrival of a European and his Wife.

[Text, vol. iii. p. 207.] While the Emperor was encamped on the Beyah, letters arrived from Khán-jahán, accompanying the tribute from Bengal, and from Rájá Mál Gosain, the *zamindár* of Kúch, who had renewed his demonstration of obedience to the Imperial throne. The tribute of Bengal consisted of the choicest productions of Bengal, and of fifty-four elephants. Along with these came a European, named Partáb Bár, one of the chief merchants of the ports of Bengal, who was accompanied by Basúrbá,[1] his wife; he was graciously received at Court, and his sound sense and upright conduct won the favour and esteem of the Emperor.

Discussions in the 'Ibádat-Khána.

(See Vol. V. p. 526.)

[Text, vol. iii. p. 215.] When the capital was illumined by the return of the Imperial presence, the old regulations came again into operation, and the house of wisdom shone resplendent on Friday nights with the light of holy minds. On the 20th Mír, in that place of meeting, the lamp was kindled to brighten the solitude of seclusion in the banquet of society, and the merits of the philosophers of the colleges and monasteries were put to the test of the touchstone. *Súfís*, doctors, preachers, lawyers, *Sunnis*, *Shí'as*, Brahmans, Jains, Buddhists, *Chár-báks*,[2] Christians, Jews, Zoroastrians, and learned men of every belief, were gathered together in the royal assembly, and were filled with delight. Each one fearlessly brought forward his assertions

[1] These names are very doubtful.
[2] *Chárvákas*, Hindú materialists.

and arguments, and the disputations and contentions were long and heated. Every sect, in its vanity and conceit, attacked and endeavoured to refute the statements of their antagonists.[1] * * * One night the *'Ibádat-Khána* was brightened by the presence of Padre Radalf,[2] who for intelligence and wisdom was unrivalled among Christian doctors. Several carping and bigoted men attacked him, and this afforded an opportunity for a display of the calm judgment and justice of the assembly! These men brought forward the old received assertions, and did not attempt to arrive at truth by reasoning. Their statements were torn to pieces, and they were nearly put to shame; and then they began to attack the contradictions in the Gospel, but they could not prove their assertions. With perfect calmness and earnest conviction of the truth, the Padre replied to their arguments, and then he went on to say, "If these men have such an opinion of our Book, and if they believe the Kurán to be the true word of God, then let a furnace be lighted, and let me with the Gospel in my hand, and the *'ulamá* with their holy book in their hands, walk into that testing place of truth, and the right will be manifest." The black-hearted mean-spirited disputants shrank from this proposal, and answered only with angry words. This prejudice and violence greatly annoyed the impartial mind of the Emperor, and, with great discrimination and enlightenment, he said: "Man's outward profession and the mere letter of Muhammadanism, without a heartfelt conviction, can avail nothing. I have forced many Brahmans, by fear of my power, to adopt the religion of my ancestors; but now that my mind has been enlightened with the beams of truth, I have become

[1] Here, and in other parts of this chapter, there are in the MSS. long passages which are not printed in the Lucknow edition. Among the rest, that about the Padre.

[2] There can be little doubt, as Mr. Blochmann has suggested, that Rodolph is the true reading; but one of my MSS. reads "*Radíf*," and the other "*Raunak*," a known word having been substituted for an unknown in each case. The translation used by Mr. Elphinstone has "Radíf." The person intended was Padre Rodolpho Aquaviva, a missionary from Goa.—See Blochmann's *Áín-i Akbari*, vol. i. p. 167; Murray's *Historical Account of Discoveries and Travels in Asia*, vol. ii.

convinced that the dark clouds of conceit and the mist of self-opinion have gathered round you, and that not a step can be made in advance without the torch of proof. That course only can be beneficial which we select with clear judgment. To repeat the words of the Creed, to perform circumcision, or to lie prostrate on the ground from dread of kingly power, can avail nothing in the sight of God:

Obedience is not in prostration on the earth:
Practise sincerity, for righteousness is not borne upon the brow."

Twenty-fifth Year of the Reign.

A Census.

[Text, vol. iii. p. 324.] An Imperial mandate was issued directing the *jágirdárs*, *shikkdars*, and *dárogahs* throughout the Empire to draw up, village by village, lists of all the inhabitants, specifying their names and occupations; and that these lists should all be collected together. The officers were not to allow any one to reside who was not engaged in some business or occupation, and they were to inquire into the arrival and departure of clever men, and ascertain whether their designs were good or evil, so that in a short time the true characters of the outwardly respectable and inwardly malicious might be brought to the test. This regulation was the means of establishing tranquillity, and of providing security for the broad expanse of Hindústán.

Twenty-seventh Year of the Reign.

Revenue Regulations.

[Text, vol. iii. p. 368.] At the beginning of this year, His Majesty directed his attention to an improvement of the administration of his territories, and passed new laws for the management of civil and revenue business. Rájá Todar Mal had, previous to this, been named as *wazír;* but the dangers and difficulties of the post, and the opposition to be encountered, made him unwilling to accept the office. But this unambitious man, who was acquainted with all the mysteries of administration, was now elevated to the office of *díwán*, and in reality to the *wakálat*. His clear judgment soon set matters to rights. Civil and revenue matters received his especial attention. Careful to keep himself free from all selfish ambition, he devoted himself to the service of the State, and earned an everlasting fame. He devoted his skill and powerful mind to simplify the laws of the State, and he allowed no grasping and intriguing men to obtain any influence over him. He now proposed several new laws calculated to give vigour and glory to the government.

That the collectors of the *khálisa* lands and the *jágírdárs* should realize[1] the *mál* and *jihát* (cesses), according to the *dastúru-l 'amal;* and if by fraud or oppression anything beyond the settled amount should be received from the cultivators, they were to account it an excess of the proper payment, and were to levy a fine upon those who had exacted it, and enter the amount in the monthly accounts. At every harvest they were to carefully guard the rights of the lower classes. These cases of giving and taking were dealt with in two ways;—the complainant received redress, and power was given to punish the offenders.

The *'ámils* of the *khálisa* had two subordinates, a *kárkun* (manager), and a *kháss-navís* (accountant). These officers had been oppressors, and leaguing with the rich, they had been a great source of evil to the poor. If instead of these two infamous officials, one worthy and honest man should be appointed, the country would prosper, and the people would be contented.

It had been discovered that in the *khálisa* districts, the cultivated lands decreased year by year; but if the lands capable of cultivation were once measured, they would increase year by year in proportion to the powers of the *raiyats;* and engagements should be made for them according to rule. The *raiyats* having

[1] The word used is *báz-yáft*, "resumption." Its meaning here seems to be that the totals were to be "brought back" to the settled standard.

nominated each other as sureties, were to take the proper writings, and in all questions of arrears were to be treated in a considerate manner.

For lands which had lain waste four years, they were to receive a deduction of one-half for the first year, for the second year one-quarter, and for the third year they were to pay according to established rule. For lands which had lain untilled for two years they were to receive a deduction of one-fourth for the first year. For uncultivated lands, they were to receive a small allowance of grain, so as to make the lands capable of yielding revenue. When advances were made for the assistance of poor cultivators, engagements were to be taken from men of respectability, and part was to be repaid at the spring harvest, part at the autumnal harvest. By these arrangements, the country would in a short period become cultivated, the *raiyats* would be contented, and the treasury flourishing. When the collectors increased the assessment, back payments were not to be required from small and insignificant estates.

Every year a report was to be made to the Emperor by the collectors, so that efficient officers might receive augmentations of their pay, and an increase of their honours and rewards; while those who did not faithfully discharge their duties would incur punishment and fall into disgrace.

When a portion of cultivated land was fixed upon, some surveyors, in proportion to its extent, were to be appointed. They were first to measure the land, and were then to acquaint themselves with its quality and produce. (The collectors) were to select a central spot for their residence. They were to carry out their duties everywhere diligently, and to inquire into the state of affairs. In seasons when a sufficient quantity of rain fell, and the lands received adequate irrigation, two and a half *biswas* (in the *bigha*) were to be left unassessed; in jungles and sandy lands, three *biswas* were to be left. Weekly accounts of sequestrations, and daily accounts of the collections, were to be sent monthly to the Imperial Exchequer. An Imperial order was issued, that when lands suffered under any visitation of Providence, a description of them was to be drawn up, and a copy of it sent to Court, so that the Emperor might give directions appropriate to the case.

If the occupants of hill forts, trusting in the security of their fastnesses, should engage in freebooting, the generals, the *faujdars*, the feudatories, and the revenue collectors were directed to unite and effect a remedy. They were first to admonish the offenders, and if that proved unavailing, they were to take measures for inflicting chastisement upon them. Their country was to be laid waste, and the land was to be granted to *jágírdárs*, from whom the revenue officers were to make no demands. If the Imperial troops received any injury, a fine was to be imposed upon the offenders.

Whatever was levied from the *raiyats* was to be paid over to the treasurers, and they were to give receipts to the *raiyats*. The collectors were to remit the payments four times a month, and at the end of this time no balance was to be left unrealized from the *raiyats*. The *raiyats* were to be so treated that they should be willing to make their payments to the treasury voluntarily. Satisfactory security was to be taken from the disaffected and contumacious; and if the bail was not given, watchmen were to be placed over the crops, and the revenue was to be realized.

A descriptive account was to be drawn up of the assessment of each individual, according to his cultivation and labour, and the dates were not to be either postponed or anticipated. The *patwári* (accountant) of each village was to apportion [the village] name by name, among the various subordinate agents, and the collectors were to send the cash under the seal of the *patwári* to the treasurer. They were to be vigilant to prevent oppression, and to treat each individual according to his deserts. The treasurer was to draw up a statement of the *mohurs*, *rupees*, and *dáms* according to the value indicated by their respective names and impressions, and showing the value of the old coinages in the new royal coins, so that the collectors and *sarráfs* might be able to ascertain the respective values of old and new coins. The *La'l-i Jalálí* of full weight and perfect touch was of the value of 400 *dáms*. The *Chahár-goshah* (four-cornered) rupee was worth forty *dáms*. The ordinary (*dastúrí*) *ashrafi* and the Akbar-sháhí rupee, which had become deteriorated in use, were to be taken at the following rates. If the *ashrafí* was only two *birinj* (grains of rice) deficient, it was to be deemed of full value, and to be received as equal to 360 *dáms*. If it was deficient from three *birinj* to one *surkh*, it was to be reckoned at 355 *dáms;* if deficient from a *surkh* to a *surkh* and a half, at 350 *dáms*. The rupee not more than one *surkh* deficient was to be considered of full value, and worth 39 *dáms*. If deficient one and a half to two *surkhs*, it was worth 38 *dáms*. The *La'l-i Jalálí* of proper touch and just weight; the *Jalála* rupee not more than from one and a half to two *surkhs* deficient; old rupees of the Akbar-sháhí coinage which might not be deficient more than from three *birinj* to one *surkh;* were to be received at the treasury. Those of greater deficiency were to be tested separately by the cashier, the particulars of them were to be entered by the accountants in their day-books, and accounts of them were to be sent every day to the Government record office. The *jágírdárs*, treasurers, and *sarráfs* (money-changers) were to act upon the above-mentioned rules. The officers of the *khálisa* and the *jágírdárs* were to make proper reports about the well-conducted and the ill-conducted, the obedient and the refractory people in their jurisdictions, so that they might get their deserts, and that the tranquillity of the country might be secured. Instead of the former expenses (*kharch*), the amount having been settled at one *dám* for each *bígha* of cultivated land, it was hoped that, upon this principle, 24 *dáms* might be the estimated sum to be allowed for each cultivator.[1]

[1] ازاین وجه بیست و چهار دام بکشت وکارسمایان مرحمت شود

Twenty-eighth Year of the Reign.

Third Conquest of Bengal.

(See Vol. V. p. 427.)

[Text, vol. iii. p. 390.] In the previous year Khán-i 'Azam Mirzá Koka received the Imperial commands to put aside his work of punishing the rebels of Bihár, and to devote his energies to the conquest of Bengal. By good fortune, the rebels of Bihár had been put to flight before the arrival of the Imperial forces. But the rainy season came on, and the campaign was deferred for that year. When the rains subsided, Sádik Khán, Shaikh Ibráhím, and Shaikh Faríd Bukhárí took their departure from Court. Officers were also sent by different roads to all the chiefs of Illahábás, Oudh, and Bihár. In a short time a large force was collected in Hájípúr, and was eager for the advance. Khán-i 'Azam, with an escort of chosen troops, proceeded by way of Garhí. Tarsún Khán * * and others crossed over the river to co-operate on the other side, but being greatly impeded by the abundance of trees, ravines, and water and mud, they recrossed the river and joined the army near Mongír. Tarsún Khán and * * then went forward one or two stages in advance. The rebels occupied a position near Káli-gang, and were prepared to fight. Mirzá Sharfu-d dín Husain, Bábá Khán Kákshál, and many other leading rebels were dead, so Ma'súm Kábulí had succeeded to the command. Katlú Lohání headed the rebels in Orissa, and part of Bengal also was in his power. On hearing of the advance of the Imperial army, Ma'súm Kábulí fell back towards Katlú, with whom he entered into negociations, and succeeded in obtaining a promise of support in men and munitions, when the Imperial forces should arrive. After making this agreement, Ma'súm hastened to Ghorá-ghát and won over Jabbári, Mirzá Beg, and all the Káksháls. To give them a feeling of security, he left his family and children at their abodes. He himself, with a body of rebels, proceeded to the Káli-gang,[1] and there made ready for battle.

[1] Two copies write Káti-gang.

On the 9th Farwardín, the advanced force of the Imperial army made an easy capture of Garhí, which is the gate of that part of the country. The *amirs* pushed on, and, fortune favouring them, they, on the 16th, came in sight of the enemy, and arrayed their forces for action. They placed batteries on the banks of the Káli-gang, and made ready their war-boats. As the generals were apprehensive of an attack from Katlú, they detached 4000 horse, under the command of Wazír Khán, towards Balkana, and this force went about twelve *kos* from the Imperial camp, to watch the movements of the enemy and guard against surprise.

Skirmishes with muskets and bows went on, and some valiant deeds were performed. But the idle talk and timid suggestions of ignorant people began to take effect upon the leaders of the army. The strength of the enemy's force was greatly exaggerated. So an application was made to the Emperor for reinforcements. The Emperor expressed his opinion that news of victory would soon arrive, but he directed Mirzá Khán, Zain Khán Koka, and * * many others to march eastwards with additional forces. But before they were ready to march, intelligence arrived of victory, and of the flight of the enemy. * * *

The Imperial army had been lying nearly a month in face of the enemy, and interchanges of cannonade and musketry went on daily. Deeds of valour were shown on either side, but a panic at length fell upon the enemy, and the royal army obtained the victory on the 4th of the month. The enemy then fled and dispersed. While a warm action was going on, Kází-záda, a leading man among the rebels, arrived from Fathábád, bringing with him many war-boats and supplies of munitions. He was struck dead by a cannon-ball. Ma'súm Khán then ordered Kálá Pahár, a distinguished rebel, to take his place; but he soon met with the same fate. Dissensions arose among the enemy, and Ma'súm Khán, the Kákshál clan, and Khálidín distrusted each other. The Imperial *amirs* took advantage of this disunion. Khálidín was first won over, and induced to take the oath of allegiance. Mirzá Beg Kákshál and Jabbárí also made terms, secretly engaging not to fight any more, and to proceed homewards. After a few days they came into the Imperial camp. The enemy being greatly downcast and discouraged, took to flight. 'Azam Khán endeavoured to pursue them, but his efforts were countervailed by the faint-hearted and frivolous objections of some of his officers. So the discomfited enemy made his escape. When the news of this victory reached the Court, orders were given to stop the march of the reinforcements.

Ma'súm, after his defeat, fled to the home of the Kákshála, in order to save his family and children from harm, now that there was ill-feeling between him and the Kákshála. Mirzá Muhammad Kákshál received him in a friendly spirit; but the Kákshála in general had posted their forces about Ghorá-ghát, and were prepared to fight. Ma'súm plundered Ghorá-ghát, and was about to attack the Kákshála. But Khán-i 'Azam sent * * with about 4000 horse, under the command of Tarsún Khán. He arrived, just as matters were going hard with the Kákshála, defeated the enemy, and drove him to Ghorá-ghát. Mirzá Beg, Khálidín, Wazír Jamíl, and others renewed their promises, and went away from the royal camp.

* * After this defeat of Ma'súm Khán, the royal forces prepared to march against Katlú, but Khán-i 'Azam had suffered from the climate, and sought to be relieved of his command. The royal order was for one of the *amirs* to take command of the army and the management of the country for a few days; and either to return to Bihár or stay where they were. Shortly afterwards, on the 8th Khurdád, Sháhbáz Khán was appointed to the command.

Burning of Widows.

[Text, vol. iii. p. 395.] In the interior of Hindústán it is the custom, when a husband dies, for his widow willingly and cheerfully to cast herself into the flames (of the funeral pile), although she may not have lived happily with him. Occasionally love of life holds her back, and then the husband's relations assemble, light the pile, and place her upon it, thinking that they thereby preserve the honour and character of the family. But since the country had come under the rule of his gracious Majesty, inspectors had been appointed in every city and district, who were to watch carefully over these two cases, to discriminate between them, and to prevent any woman being forcibly burnt. About this time, Jai Mál (son of Mál Deo), who had been sent with his forces to join the *amírs* in Bengal, died of sunstroke in the vicinity of Chaunsá. His wife, the daughter of Múna Rájá, was unwilling to burn; but her son Udí Singh, with a party of his bigoted friends, resolved upon the sacrifice. The matter came to the Emperor's knowledge, and his feeling of justice and humanity made him fear that if he sent messengers to stop the proceedings, some delay might occur, so he mounted his horse, and rode with all speed to the place. As the facts were not fully known, some of these men, in their thoughtlessness, were disposed to resist and make disturbances. * * But when His Majesty arrived, Jagganáth and Rái Sál came forward to meet him, and brought the leader of these foolish men to him. He accepted their assurance of repentance, and only placed them in confinement.

Katlú in Orissa.

(See Vol. V. p. 429.)

[Text, vol. iii. p. 401.] When Shaikh Faríd escaped from Katlú and reached the Imperial camp, the *amírs* started from their lethargy and crossed the river Damodar,[1] and marched for two *kos* in battle array. Katlú entrenched his camp, and prepared to hold out. There also many others took refuge with him. In another place, was Bahádur with a separate force. At the new moon of Amurdád, Sádik Khán and Sháh Kulí Khán attacked him, and broke into his entrenchments, when he fled to join Katlú. Next day the Imperial troops followed; and when they came in

[1] Which falls into the Hoogly, near its mouth.

sight of his position, they mounted some guns on the neighbouring heights. These proceedings alarmed the enemy, who fled to Orissa. The Imperial leaders had not resolution and enterprise enough to pursue, but came to a halt by the river.

Burhánu-l Mulk comes to Court.

(See Vol. V. p. 429.)

[Text, vol. iii. p. 401.] Burhánu-l Mulk was the younger brother of Murtazá Nizámu-l Mulk. When Husain Nizámu-l Mulk died, the Nizámu-l Mulkí kingdom descended to his eldest son, but in reality the government fell into the hands of the young prince's mother. He, like his father before him, preferred Burhán to all his friends. In course of time, designing persons stirred up strife between him and his relations, so that he seized and sent to a fortress both his mother and his brother. His ignorance and vicious propensities kept him aloof from the loyal and good, and threw him into the company of evil persons, whose bad advice quite perverted his mind. He raised a low fellow, a cock-fighter named Husain, to be his companion, and foolishly gave him the title of Ásaf Khán. * * This low-born fellow stirred up a war against Bidar, and a fierce struggle went on in Kandahár.[1] The news of these foolish proceedings soon spread abroad, and Burhán, having escaped from prison by the aid of his keeper, began to raise disturbances; but his mind was in fetters, and his fortune asleep. He cast his eyes upon the wealth of others, and began to oppress them. When Nizámu-l Mulk was informed of this outbreak, he hastened back, and reached Ahmadnagar on the day he desired. * * Numbers of men deserted Burhán, and he was obliged to fly without fighting. He then went to 'Ádil Khán at Bíjanagar (*sic*). Not being able to effect anything there, he went in the disguise of a *jogí* to Ahmadnagar. There he lived in secret, and endeavoured to raise a party among the evil-disposed. Being discovered, he hastened to the governor of Baglána, and not being able to effect anything there, he went

[1] Sixty miles north of Bidar.

to Kutbu-d dín Khán, at Bidar. From thence he proceeded to the Imperial Court, where he met with a gracious reception. [*Account of the impostor who had preceded him.*—See Vol. V. p. 429.]

Defeat of Ma'súm Kábulí by Sháhbáz Khán.

[Text, vol. iii. p. 412.] After the defeat of the rebels, a portion of the victorious forces marched towards Orissa, and encamped by the river Damodar. There they rested, and a detachment was sent to Ghorá-ghát, to secure the safety of the Kákshâls. After some time, Ma'súm Khán, at the head of a strong rebel force, came out of the country of Bhátí against Mirzá Beg Kákshál, who sought refuge with Tarsún Khán at Tájpúr. Ma'súm detached parties to plunder the neighbourhood, and Tarsún Khán shut himself up in the fort. The country was overrun to within seven *kos* of Tánda. When Sháhbáz Khán was informed of this, he marched to inflict punishment on the rebel. An advanced force was sent on with all speed, and he himself marched from Patna with his army. He proceeded by land, and in a short time reached the disturbed districts, and the rebels fell back before him. Ma'súm Khán was near the Jumna, and there he rested. Sháhbáz wrote from Tánda to the *amír* who held Orissa, saying, that Katlú had no longer the courage to face the royal army, and that they should send a portion of their forces to support himself. Accordingly Wazír Khán and * * joined Sháhbáz Khán. That officer then crossed the Ganges, when he was providentially joined by 3000 artillerymen from Bhátí, who had been in the service of Sháh Bardí, then lately deceased. This reinforcement raised great hopes of victory, and was attached to the divisions of Tarsún Khán and Mirzá Beg Kákshál. Sháh Kulí Khán, and two or three other chiefs of distinction, came and joined the royal army. Intelligence was now brought that Bábá Bhakarí, with a rebel force, had gone to the town of Santús, and defeated Tarsún Khán. Sháhbáz Khán sent a detachment under Muhibb 'Alí Khán to support Tarsún, and he himself quickly followed. The enemy then fled, and much spoil fell into the hands of the royal forces. Ma'súm Khán, knowing the crossing of the river to be a difficult operation, took up a position on the bank of the Jumna, opposite the Imperial army. [*Negociations.*] Sháhbáz Khán at length cut short the negociations, and crossed the river mid a storm of arrows and bullets. The action soon grew warm, and the rebels were beaten, and put to flight, on the 4th Ázur. The boats of the Imperial fleet did not arrive to take part in the fight; but Náráin Búmí and Murád Kákshál brought up their vessels, and contributed to the victory. Muhibb 'Alí Khán was sent in pursuit of the fugitives; but a party of them rallied, and gave battle to the pursuers. Sháhbáz, hearing of this check, marched on to retrieve it. Another sharp battle was fought, in which the enemy was again defeated, and [Ma'súm] Farankhúdí was made prisoner. Much spoil was secured, and the foe fled in confusion. Mirzá Beg, and Sangrám, and Dalpat rendered effective assistance. The royal forces pursued the fugitives over rivers and through marshes to Ghorá-ghát, which was once more plundered. Ma'súm Khán fled with a few followers to Bhátí, and Jabbárí to Kúch. About 150 men were taken prisoners.

Twenty-ninth Year of the Reign.

Operations against Ma'súm Khán.

[Text, vol. iii. p. 432.] After the defeat of Ma'súm Khán, Sháhbáz Khán went on after him towards Bhátí, regardless of the rains and the swollen rivers. 'Ísá Khán, the ruler of that country, professed to be a loyal adherent of the Imperial throne. Sháhbáz Khán now determined to test this by calling upon him to surrender Ma'súm Khán, resolving also to tear the veil from his face, and punish him if he refused. Bhátí is a low-lying country, and is called by that Hindí name,[1] because it lies lower than Bengal. It extends nearly 400 *kos* from east to west, and

[1] *Bháthí*, "down the stream."

nearly 300 from south to north. On the east lies the sea and the country of Jessore; on the west lies the hill country south of Tánda;[1] on the north the salt sea, and the extremities of the hills of Tibet. The father of the chief of this country was a man of the Bais tribe of Rájpúts, who used frequently to display his arrogance, and break out in rebellion. In the times of Salím Khán, Táj Khán, and Daryá Khán, strong armies were sent into the country, and after a severe struggle, the chief was compelled to seek a truce. After a short time, he again broke out in rebellion, but was taken prisoner and put to death. His two sons, 'Ísá and Isma'íl, were sold to merchants. When Salím Khán died, and Táj Khán seized upon the country of Bengal, Kutb Khán, the uncle of 'Ísá, won distinction by his good service. By great exertions, he brought the two brothers out of the country of Túrán. 'Ísá, by his intelligence and prudence, acquired a name, and he made twelve *zamíndárs* of Bengal to become his dependents. By his foresight and adroitness, he continually professed his allegiance to the rulers of Bengal, and sent his tribute; but he took care not to see them.

The army of Sháhbáz Khán reached the banks of the Ganges, near Khizrpúr. This is a place, where there is a ferry over the river, and consequently two strong forts had been built there, one on each side of the river. He soon made himself master of these strongholds, and occupied the village of Sunárgánw. Next he took Katrápúr, where the magazines were, and plundered it. His army next marched rapidly to a large city called Mashhadí, where great plunder was obtained. After this, they encamped on the shores of the Brahmaputra, which is a large river that flows from Khatá. Ma'súm Khán fled before the advanced force, and took refuge in an island, being very nearly taken prisoner. Meantime 'Ísá, who had been away in Kúch, arrived with a large force and excellent supplies. The Imperial officers then

[1] کوهستان بنگاه کروه کهن جنوب تانده. Perhaps و may be inserted before *junúb*: it will then read "on the south Tánda." But the whole description is unintelligible.—See Blochmann's *Ain-i Akbari*, vol. i. p. 342.

took post at Totak, on the bank of the Brahmaputra, opposite the town of Kumára-samundar, and fortified their position. They were warmly attacked, both by land and water, but on each occasion obtained a fresh victory. Tarsún Khán was now detached to distract the enemy, by menacing an attack upon their supplies at Bajrápúr. There were two roads from Bhowál:[1] one at a distance from the enemy's position, the other along the river bank pretty close to it. By the decree of fate, Tarsún Khán chose the latter route, and Ma'súm, being apprised of this, marched to attack him with a large force. Sháhbáz Khán sent Muhibb 'Alí Khán and * * with swift messengers to apprise Tarsún of his danger, and to direct him to take up a strong position, and not to fight till he received reinforcements. * * On being informed that a force was approaching, Tarsún Khán, casting prudence aside, inferred that it was his reinforcements, and went forth to meet and welcome them. He had not proceeded far, when he discovered that they were enemies. His friends advised him to return to his camp, gather his own men around him, and wait for the reinforcements; but it was of no avail. With a bold and daring heart he prepared for the fight. Part of his followers left him; but with no more than fifteen who remained true, he gave battle. Two of his relatives were slain fighting bravely, and he himself was taken prisoner. Ma'súm received him with a great show of kindness and friendship, and endeavoured to win him over; but his advances were repulsed with scorn and reproof. This woke the narrow-minded rebel from his dream, and stirred up his wrath, so that he slew Tarsún Khán, full of years and of imperishable fame.

Katlú Kirání.

[Text, vol. iii. p. 436.] When Sháhbáz Khán marched against Bhátí, a force was sent under Wazír Khán to Burdwan, against Katlú. But the time was passed in doing nothing, until Sádik Khán arrived. He was an active and intelligent officer, and

[1] North of Dacca.

soon worked a change. The rebel fled in shame to Orissa, and the Imperial officers pursued him to Takarohí, where he was so pressed that he was obliged to seek refuge in the forests of Dharmpúr. Unwilling to molest him farther, and weary of the campaign, the *amirs* renewed to him the former offer of allowing him to remain ruler of Orissa, as a tributary of the Empire. He accepted the terms, sent his nephew to Court to express his allegiance and duty, and made an offering of sixty choice elephants.

Sháhbáz Khán's failure at Bháti.

[Text, vol. iii. p. 437.] Sháhbáz Khán occupied a position on the Panár river, a branch of the Brahmaputra. Here he entered into negociations with the rebels, in the expectation of being able to win them over to his views. 'Ísá received his propositions very respectfully, and for a time kept up communications. But it became apparent that his words and his intentions were not in unison, and so the war again began. For seven months the Imperial forces obtained victories from time to time, and the rebels were disheartened by failure. But Sháhbáz Khán, in his self-conceit, had paid little regard to the feelings of the *amirs* in his army. They combined to thwart him, and ill-feeling waxed powerful. Death was busy among them, and their position became insupportable. The enemy knew that the Imperial army was dispirited, and although, by good fortune, there had been little rain, the men were listless and in low spirits. The enemy brought up a number of labourers, and cut the banks of the Brahmaputra in fifteen places, and turned the waters into the Imperial camp. When the batteries were flooded, they brought up to them large boats, called in the language of the country *biyára*. A fire of cannons and musketry was opened on both sides, and suddenly a great stroke of fortune happened to the Imperial forces, when a musket-ball from their ranks killed the commander of the assailants. Some of the boats came in collision, and suddenly the waters began to fall. This compelled them to take flight, and many of their men were drowned. They were defeated on all sides, except in the battery of Saiyid Husain, *thánádár* of Dacca, who was taken prisoner.

'Ísá now awoke from his dream of ignorance, and opened communications through the medium of this prisoner. Sháhbáz Khán received his overtures favourably, and 'Ísá consented to submit to the supremacy of the Emperor, and to acknowledge himself a servant. The port of Sunárgánw was to receive an Imperial *dárogha*. Ma'súm was to be sent on the pilgrimage to Mecca, and tribute was to be transmitted to the Emperor. He won the hearts of the *amírs* by his munificent presents, and the royal army retired.

Sháhbáz Khán crossed the river, and reached the confines of Bhowál, looking for the fulfilment of the agreement; but the mind of 'Ísá had been perverted by evil counsellors. He now made new propositions and conditions, which led to sharp contentions. Preparations for renewing the war went on, and on the 19th Mihr he offered battle. The *amírs* in the royal army were so short-sighted and weak in judgment, that they looked for their own advantage in the failure of Sháhbáz Khán, and thought to profit by his defeat. The first to leave him was Muhibb 'Alí Khán, and he was followed by others, who each pursued his own course. Sháh Kulí Khán Mahram made a stand against the enemy; but he was wounded, and was ill-supported by his men, so he evacuated Bhowál. Sháhbáz Khán now awoke to his danger, and endeavoured to conciliate his officers; but his repentance was too late, and he was compelled to retreat towards Tánda, abandoning his baggage. The sons of the *Mír-i 'adl*, and many others were taken prisoners, and Shaikh Muhammad Ghazniví and several others were drowned. * * After eight days' retreat, the army rested to take breath at Sherpúr. Sháhbáz Khán now endeavoured to collect his forces, with the intention of returning to avenge his defeat; but his followers were incensed with him, and refused to support him. On reaching Tánda, Wazír Khán came forward loyally to support him.

But Sháhbáz showed his old temper, and they could not come to any agreement; so Sháhbáz was compelled to proceed to Court. As soon as the news reached the Emperor, he sent officers to stop the return of the unsuccessful chiefs, and to administer counsel and reproof. Sa'íd Khán, and other *jágírdárs* of Bihár and Bengal, were directed to join with their forces, and to aid in the punishment of the rebellious *samíndár*. * *

'Ísá was too cautious to leave his own country, but he induced Ma'súm to advance to Sherpúr. A detachment of the rebels overran the country as far as Málda, and to within twelve *kos* of Tánda. Wazír Khán did not feel sufficient confidence to go out and attack them; but he held his ground, and secured that important city. The royal messengers now arrived, and turned Sháhbáz Khán back with words of censure. He was told that if more forces were necessary, Rájá Todar Mal and other chiefs should be ordered to join him; but he replied that his army was now numerous, and the men full of ardour. On the 18th De, he entered Bengal, intent on the conquest of Bhátí, and the rebels retreated before him. On reaching the Jumná,[1] he learnt that Ma'súm was at Sherpúr, and did not expect that his opponents would cross the river. Sháhbáz Khán immediately determined to cross the river and advance; but the *amírs* dissented from his design. However, he skilfully conveyed some troops over this great river, and immediately upon their approach the enemy fled, leaving many prisoners and much spoil behind them. * * * Sa'íd Khán and * * went in pursuit of the enemy, who fell back as he approached. After the country was clear of the rebels, the *amírs* returned to Sherpúr Míraja. * *

While the Imperial forces were at Sherpúr, Ma'súm Khán proceeded towards Fathábád in Orissa, and Dastam Khán Kákshál also remained in that neighbourhood, in the hope that if the Imperial army were divided, he might find an opportunity of striking a blow, and before any intelligence was received about Ma'súm, this rebel (Dastam Khán) had overrun the country to

[1] See next note *infrà*.

within twelve *kos* of the Imperial camp. A force was sent against him, before which he retired. [*Dissensions of Sháhbáz Khán and the 'amírs.*]

At length it was agreed that as the enemy had two armies, the Imperial forces should also be divided. One under Wazír Khán and * * was to march against Ma'súm; while Sháhbáz Khán and * * remained where they were, to watch over and keep in check the rebels of that quarter. * *

Thirtieth Year of the Reign.

Rebels in Bengal.

[Text, vol. iii. p. 466.] Ma'súm Khán, on hearing of the approach of the royal forces, made new preparations. Having selected a strong position, he proceeded to erect fortifications at Taramhání, a place where the Ganges, the Jumná, and the Sáktí unite.[1] There he founded two forts. When the Imperial *amírs* had made the needful preparations, the wary 'Ísá endeavoured to make terms; but his proposals were not listened to. The *amírs* resolved to attack the fortifications, and commenced operations, driving the enemy before them. On the 21st Farwardín, one of the forts was assaulted and taken with the help of boats, and the other was captured on the following morning. They then attacked Ma'súm, who, being unable to check their advance, made his escape by the river.

While the *amírs* entertained expectations of 'Ísá proving true to his engagements, they directed their attention towards Orissa, where Sulaimán Sarbaní had broken out in revolt; and having gathered many Afgháns around him, was plundering the country. They attacked the son of Wazír Khán in the neighbourhood of Burdwan, and after a sharp action, compelled him to shut himself up in that place. The Imperial *amírs* hastened to his relief, and the rebels being compelled to raise the siege, took up a position

1 "Some leagues below Dacca, the river (Ganges) separates into two branches. One, called Padmávatí, runs eastward, and falls into the sea at Chittagong. The other branch runs northward, and divides into three streams, called Sarsuti, Jumná, and Ganges."—*Árdish-i Mahfil.*

on the banks of the river Mangal-kot.[1] * * Sádik Khán attacked them, and defeated them. * * Three hundred of them fell in the action, and a thousand in the pursuit. * *

At the time the Imperial *amírs* retired from Bengal to Bihár, Dastam Kákshál laid siege to Ghorá-ghát. Bábú Mangalí now came up from Sherpúr Míraja, and compelled him to raise the siege.

Pacification of Bengal.

[Text, vol. iii. p. 490.] When the Emperor marched to the Panjáb, he received intelligence that Wazír was unable by himself to secure tranquillity in Bengal, and that the rebels were still active. Orders were accordingly sent to Sháhbáz Khán, directing him to march from Bihár to Bengal. Although Sháhbáz requested to be allowed to return to Court, messengers were sent to him with positive instructions to proceed on this duty. The messengers reached him at Jaunpúr, and on the 20th Bahman, he proceeded to carry out his duties in Bengal. By conciliation and judicious encouragement he won over the rebels, so that they submitted and became peaceful. A detachment was sent to the country of Bhátí against 'Ísá, and the territory abandoned by Sádik Khán was recovered. 'Ísá humbly submitted, and sent presents to the Imperial Court. Ma'súm Khán had entered so deeply into rebellion, that he was afraid to present himself; but he offered to send his son in token of submission to the Imperial Court, while he himself lived quietly in seclusion. It was determined that the best thing he could do would be to proceed to Mecca, and afterwards go to Court. Many of the Afgháns of Katlú left him and joined the royal forces. Katlú himself made specious representations, and Sháhbáz Khán was simple enough to give back Orissa to him.

At this time, a force was detached against Kokra,[2] a flourishing country lying between Orissa and the Dakhin. Mádhú

[1] Eighteen miles north of Burdwan.

[2] کوکره Khoorda?

Singh Búmí the chief, relying upon the difficulties of the approach over the mountains, offered resistance. The Imperial forces, however, made good their approach, overran the country and made it tributary.

Defeat of the Imperial Forces.—Death of Rájá Bírbal.

[Text, vol. iii. p. 494.] When Kokaltásh (Zain Khán) marched to effect the subjugation of Swád (Swát) and Bajaur, he first subdued Bajaur, in which he found 30,000 houses of the Yúsufzáí tribe. * * He then marched against Swát, in which mountain region there were 40,000 houses of the same tribe. On reaching the banks of the river, the natives made a strenuous resistance, and the advanced guard was checked for a time; but the braves of the *altamsh* went to their support, and the sight of their gallantry so encouraged the rest, that they fought bravely, and put the enemy to flight. Kokaltásh built a fort at Jag-dara, in the midst of the country, and then applied himself to the chastisement of the enemy. Twenty-three times he was victorious, and he destroyed seven armies. All the country was brought under his hand, except the hills of Karágar and the country of Bunír. But his army was worn out with ascending mountains and continual fighting; he was in consequence compelled to ask for reinforcements. The Emperor sent Rájá Bírbal, Hakím Abú-l Fath, and other officers to support him. They had no sooner arrived, than dissensions arose among them. Hard words and fierce looks were exchanged between Kokaltásh and the Rájá. The Rájá and the Hakím were also on ill terms with each other. * * When they reached the hills of Malkand, Kokaltásh endeavoured to reconcile them, and they held a long debate as to the distribution of the various forces. Hakím Abú-l Fath hastened off with some forces to the fort of Jag-dara. The Rájá was incensed at this separation, and nursed his angry feelings.

In the morning they met at the fort. Kokaltásh prepared a feast, and invited his colleagues. But the Rájá refused to attend, and sent to say, that the best thing to be done was for experienced men to meet and determine on the course to be pursued. Kokaltásh repressed his anger, and went to the Rájá. Other chiefs also went with him, and represented that it would be best to recognize Kokaltásh as chief, and meet to consult at his abode. At this council the Rájá and the Hakím spoke hotly, and then abused each other; but by the conciliatory conduct of Kokaltásh, they were appeased. * * He then proposed that a force should be left to hold the fort, while the rest of the army marched against the enemy. He thought that the fresh forces might undertake this work, while he remained with the old force to protect the centre of the country; or if they preferred, they might remain at Jag-dara, while he went to chastise the mountaineers. The Rájá and the Hakím rejected both propositions, and said it was the Emperor's desire, not that they should occupy the country, but that they should inflict chastisement on the enemy, and hasten back to Court. Kokaltásh remonstrated that it was inexpedient to abandon a country which had been acquired with such difficulty; that the attempt to return through the defiles of the mountains would be rash: if they would not agree to either course he had proposed, and were determined to return, the best plan would be to proceed by the way they had come, for that was practicable for an army, and the enemy could not stop them. They adhered to their own proposition, and Kokaltásh weakly put aside his duties as a general, lest his associates should convey their complaints to the Emperor, and excite his displeasure. They were afraid that if they marched separately, their attempts would fail, and they would incur disgrace; so fate had its way, and the word was given for the march of the whole army, and the Rájá and the Hakím received the command of the right and left wing. * *

On the 2nd Isfandármuz, they marched from Jag-dara towards Karágar, and having proceeded five *kos*, they halted at the village of Kándák. Next day the road was full of defiles, and the right wing was left as a rear-guard, while the halt was made half a *kos* in advance. The advance-guard was to skirmish a little in front for that day, and then fall back. Next morning, when the advance entered the pass, the fight began. The Imperial forces were successful in several encounters, and in a short time carried the pass, and captured some booty. Thousands were lured into this snare. The *altamsh*, also, hearing the cry of plunder, hastened to share it, and large numbers of the main body broke and hastened forward. Kokaltásh, who had chosen the camping ground, when he advanced and came in front of the Afgháns, found the troops engaged in plundering. Hasan Khán Tabatí was carried off wounded, and matters looked very serious. Kokaltásh, on learning this, engaged in the fight, and made a firm stand. That day and that night, and the early part of the next day, the battle went on. Kokaltásh shot four of the enemy's chiefs with his own hands, and the foe was for a time repulsed. The close of the day brought victory; but the baggage of the camels and oxen had been plundered. That which was carried by elephants and mules came up.

Next day they they advanced six *kos*, near to Khánpúr, and there halted. Kokaltásh himself took the command of the rear, and fighting all the way, reached the camping ground. He then repaired to the Rájá, to consult with him as to what course was to be taken, blaming the movements that had been made, and eloquently exposing his own views. As the distance before them was now diminished, and the rugged nature of the way was not visible, the general opinion was, that they should leave the hills and rest for a few days, until a plan could be formed for overpowering their adversaries. Kokaltásh represented that the ground in front of them was most difficult, and it was utterly futile to attempt it. His own opinion was, that they should stay where they were for a while and defend themselves. The space was sufficiently large; there was no danger of the foe gaining a position to command it; there was abundance of water and grass, and plenty of wood to build stockades: they might thus inflict chastisement on the fierce foes who held all the hills around. Else they might send and endeavour to make peace, by restoring the prisoners and booty they had taken, on condition of receiving hostages. Or, they might wait for a while, until news of their position reached the Emperor, and he sent an army to seize the hills from that side. But fate had ordained it otherwise. They held to their own views, and thought they saw their safety in what was to be their ruin.

On the 6th Isfandármuz, they marched towards the lofty mountain of Bulandrai. Kokaltásh wisely took command of the rear. The fighting began again more fiercely than before. When they had made some little way, and evening came on, finding a lofty mountain before them, they came to a halt. On Kokaltásh coming up, it became clear that there was another defile to pass before they could be safe. As this was governed by heights close at hand, he made haste to push forward. The advance-guard was ordered to ascend the heights and clear the commanding positions; then to come down again at a distance, and at the early dawn show the way over this difficult mountain. When they were repulsed by the Afgháns, Kokaltásh with a party of braves rallied them; but others hastened to fall back, and all order was lost. Although Kokaltásh exerted himself to re-assure them and restore order, it was all in vain. The Afgháns attacked them fiercely on every side with arrows and stones, and they were driven from the heights in disorder and dismay. At the bottom, elephants, horses, and men, were all mixed together in confusion. There many brave and noble men made a bold stand, and sold their lives. One party, having found a passage, made their escape; and at the close of the day another party made their way over the rugged mountain. Kokaltásh was with this party. In the conflict he had resolved to sell his life, but a brave friend seized his rein, and dragged him out of the fight. At length he reached the camp on foot, through a hundred difficulties. Scared and foolish men raised the cry that the Afgháns were upon them. So, in the greatest distress, they moved on from that place at an unseasonable hour. In the darkness many lost their way, and fell down precipices. The Afgháns stayed behind, securing and dividing the plunder.

Next day, many of the wanderers perished, and some were made prisoners. In this conflict 500 men perished.[1] Among them was Rájá Bírbal, whose loss the Emperor greatly deplored.

Thirty-first Year of the Reign.

Conquest of Birár.

[Text, vol. iii. p. 503.] Birár is a Rájpút state adjoining the country of Málwa. The rulers of the Dakhin did not pay proper obedience to the Imperial Government, so Khán-i 'Azam Mirzá Koka received orders to march, with a great many other *amírs*, to inflict punishment upon them. He proceeded to Hindia, to make preparations for the campaign, and a force which he sent in advance took Sánwalí-garh from Náhir Ráo. Other *zamíndárs* made offers of submission. But dissensions suddenly arose among the *amírs* of the Imperial army. The commander gave grants in Málwa to his own adherents, and the *amírs* who had been sent on the campaign had great altercations with him, so that divisions arose, and the work of the campaign was arrested. Shahábu-d dín Ahmad Khán went off in anger to his *jágír*, and instead of lending assistance, prepared for opposition. By the exertions of prudent men, a conflict was prevented; but the two *amírs* would not work together. Tolak Khán, one of the principal *amírs*, was thrown into prison on a false charge. Amír Fathu-lla Shírází received many annoyances, and retired before the ruler of Khándesh, to seek refuge with Khán-khánán in Gujarát. By unnecessary delays and dispersion of the troops, the Imperial army in a short time dwindled down, and the enemy, who before had trembled, now grew bold. Rájá 'Alí Khán of Khándesh and * * assembled the forces of Birár and Ahmadnagar, and advanced to give battle. The royal *amírs* now

[1] This must mean one particular episode of the battle, for according to the *Tabakát* nearly 8000 men fell. See Vol. V. p. 451; see also the Extract from the *Zubdatu-t Tawáríkh*, post; Elphinstone, book ix. chap. ii.

awoke from their dream, and endeavoured to form some plan, but did not know friend from foe, and could not distinguish between supporters and opponents. Vacillation and discordant counsels made all hope of unity and resistance vain; so they retired before the enemy towards Birár, leaving their baggage. On their march, they put their guide, Hathyá Ráo Búmí, to death, upon suspicion of treachery. From want of proper information, a force was sent into an intricate country, near Kherla, and suffered great loss. Finding Birár unoccupied, they plundered it, and on New Year's Day they sacked Ellichpúr, the capital of the country. One party was for going off to Ahmadnagar, another for trying to hold the country. This proposition was not listened to, and so they moved off with their plunder towards Gujarát. * * When the enemy got intelligence of the retreat, he left his artillery and heavy baggage, and marching quickly against Hindia, he plundered and burnt that town. * * The Khán-i 'Azam went off express to Gujarát, to seek the aid of the forces under Khán-khánán.

Thirty-fifth Year of the Reign.

Europeans at Court.

[Text, vol. iii. p. 602.] At this time, Padre Farmalíún[1] arrived at the Imperial Court from Goa, and was received with much distinction. He was a man of much learning and eloquence. A few intelligent young men were placed under him for instruction, so that provision might be made for securing translations of Greek books and of extending knowledge. With him came a number of Europeans and Armenians, who brought silks of China and goods of other countries, which were deemed worthy of His Majesty's inspection.

Orissa.

(See Vol. V. p. 465.)

[Text, vol. iii. p. 604.] Rájá Mán Singh, the ruler of Bihár,

[1] فرمليون

had, by his ability, reduced that province to tranquillity, and punished the rebels. So towards the end of the year, he had formed the design of invading Orissa by way of Jhárkand. He halted at Bhágalpúr, and there sent to ask for the co-operation of Sa'íd Khán, the governor of Bengal, who, in consequence of the near approach of the rainy season, postponed his assistance. At the beginning of the present year the Rájá marched by way of Bardwán, and he was accompanied by Bihár Khán and others, with artillery from Bengal. He halted at Jahánábád till the rains should be over, and Sa'íd Khán and others should come to support him. But Katlú had raised his banner in Orissa, and now boldly advanced to Dharpúr, twenty-five *kos* from the Imperial army, with the intention of giving battle. He sent forward Bahádur with a numerous force to Ráípúr; and to check this force the Rájá advanced a detachment under the command of Jaggat Singh. The rebel was obliged to take refuge in fortifications, and then submissively offered to treat; but he, at the same time, artfully called upon Katlú for support. * * Katlú sent men to his assistance. Jaggat Singh was warned of his danger, but paid no heed. At length he was attacked by the rebels, and was obliged to fly and abandon his camp; but he was saved by Hamír, the *zamíndár* who had given him warning, and conducted to Bishanpúr. Upon learning of this reverse, Rájá Mán Singh held a council, and the prevailing opinion was, that it was desirable to retreat to Salímábád, where the families of his troops were, and there to re-organize his army. But the Rájá rejected these counsels, and resolved upon taking the offensive. The Imperial good fortune now came to his aid, and the rebel Katlú died, after an illness of ten days. His younger son succeeded him, but the Afgháns sued for an arrangement. The excessive rains and the depression of the royal forces made a settlement desirable. It was accordingly agreed that the Emperor's name should be used in the *khutba* and on the coins, that the country should be obedient and loyal, that Jagganáth, the celebrated place of worship, should, with its dependencies, become subject to the royal exchequer, and that no injury should be done to the loyal *zamíndárs.* All of them, with craft and dissimulation, affixed their signatures to this document. On the 4th Shahryúr, Katlú's son was brought in, with 150 elephants and many valuable articles, which were offered as tribute. Rájá Mán Singh then returned to Bihár.

Thirty-sixth Year of the Reign.

Burhánu-l Mulk.

[Text, vol. iii. p. 612.] When Burhánu-l Mulk made his first attempt on the territory of the south, and was unsuccessful, he returned to his estates. Now that Khán-i 'Azam had gone to Gujarát, and Sháhbáz Khán was dead, he betook himself to Rájá 'Alí Khán, the ruler of Khándesh, who, in compliance with the Imperial commands, was eager to assist him. He had also agreed with 'Ádil Khán, of Bíjápúr, that a force should be sent from thence when they approached Ahmadnagar; and accordingly a contingent was sent to the frontier, to await the arrival of Rájá 'Alí's army. Jamál Khán, the governor of Ahmadnagar, resolved to prevent the junction of the two forces. Before Burhánu-l Mulk came near, Jamál Khán defeated his son Isma'íl, and then hastened to attack the forces of Bíjápúr, and defeated them with little difficulty. When, after this, Burhánu-l Mulk entered Birár, Muhammadu-l Mulk and * * other chiefs joined him. Jamál Khán, inflated with his previous victory, marched out rashly to oppose him. * * Rájá 'Alí Khán placed Burhánu-l Mulk in charge of the *amírs* of Birár, and gave battle to Jamál Khán. A sharp fight ensued; but Jamál Khán was killed by a musket-shot, and his army was broken up. A great victory was gained. Soon after, Isma'íl Khán, the son, was brought in a prisoner, and was placed in confinement. The ruler of Khándesh then led a detachment to Ahmadnagar, and soon made himself master of the whole country.

When Burhánu-l Mulk got possession of Ahmadnagar, he

had a fine opportunity of showing his gratitude and fidelity, and of making himself an example to other rulers. But the intoxication of success got the mastery over him. He forgot the many and great favours he had received, oppressed the people under him, and sought his own advantage in the wrongs of others. The Emperor determined to send first an envoy to Rájá 'Alí Khán, who had raised Burhán to the position he held, to consult with him and the other rulers of that quarter, as to whether they would invade his territories. If they agreed, the ambassador was to return; if not, an Imperial army was to be sent. Shaikh Abú-l Faiz Faizí, "the prince of poets," was accordingly sent to Rájá 'Alí Khán and Burhánu-l Mulk.

Thirty-seventh Year of the Reign.

Conquest of Orissa.

[Text, vol. iii. p. 640.] This country had always been governed by independent rulers. Among them was one named Partáb Ráo, whose son, Nar Singh, strove against him, and took an opportunity of poisoning him. Mukund Deo, a native of Telingana, and a servant of the late Rájá, rose up in opposition to the new ruler. Upon the pretence that his wife was going to pay a visit to the usurper, he sent a number of *dúlis*, filled with arms, and a number of active men as ostensible guards of his tribute. They were admitted into the fort, and soon put an end to the usurper. Although it was the rule and custom that new rulers should not expend the treasures accumulated by their predecessors, Mukund broke open seventy chests, and appropriated their contents. He was very liberal in the use of them, but his act alienated the feelings of the people.

When Sikandar Khán Uzbek left the Imperial service and joined Sulaimán Kirání, the latter sent his son, Báyazíd, by way of Jhárkand, the Benares of that country, against Orissa; and he sent Sikandar with him. The Rájá sent two of his chiefs to oppose him, but many of their men were lured by money to desert them and abandon their master. Some fighting followed, in which Mukund and his general Ishat Rái were killed. Power then fell into the hands of Rakh Banj (?), but Sulaimán got him into his power, and made an end of him. He then established his power over the whole country.

In the time of Khán-khánán Mun'im Khán and Khán-jahán, a large portion of this country had been brought under the Imperial rule; but through the incompetency of the *amírs* it had been wrested from them by Katlú Lohání. When Katlú died, and Rájá Mán Singh withdrew his forces, as before related, his course was disapproved by many wise men; but a treaty was patched up. The evil spirits of the country now strove to overthrow each other, but so long as Katlú's *vakíl* 'Ísá lived, the treaty was observed. When he died, the turbulent Afgháns seized upon the temple of Jagannáth, and plundered the country of Hamír, who had proved himself loyal.

Rájá Mán Singh regretted the treaty he had formerly made, and projected another campaign, for which he received the Imperial permission. The forces of Bengal and Bihár were named for the service. On the 23rd Ábán, he set off by water, but Tolak Khán and * * the other *amírs* proceeded by land. Mádhú and Lakhí Rái and * * other *zamíndárs* were sent by way of Jhárkand under the command of Yúsuf Khán, the ruler of Kashmír. When the army reached Bengal, Sa'íd Khán, the ruler of the province, was ill; but as the business was urgent, the Rájá pushed on without him. When Sa'íd recovered, he followed the army, and joined it with * * many chiefs and 6500 horse. A great part of the country was occupied. The crafty Afgháns sought to make peace; but experience had shown what their professions were worth, and a deaf ear was turned to their propositions, though some of the *amírs* of Bengal were in favour of an amicable settlement. The enemy took up a position in the forests of Midnapúr, a place in the middle of Orissa. [*Disposition of the royal forces.*] On the 31st Farwardín, Rájá Mán Singh ordered an advance. * * The enemy then crossed the river, and set their forces in array. Their centre, under the command of Nasíb Khán and Jamál Khán, sons of Katlú, consisted of 3000 horse, and twenty-five elephants. In the wings were 2000 horse and twenty-five elephants, and in their advance were 1200 horse and eighty elephants. Battle was joined and was well contested, the result being for some time doubtful. * * But victory declared in favour of the Imperial forces. The Afgháns had 300 men killed, and the royal army lost forty men.

Capture of Júnagarh.

(See Vol. V. p. 461.)

[Text, vol. iii. p. 651.] When Khán-i 'Azam had established his authority in Gujarát, he resolved to extend his sway, and to bring more of that region under his rule. At first he was impeded by the timidity of his followers; but after they had rested and recovered their spirits, he renewed his projects. Somnát, Koka, Mangalor, Mahú, Paro, and seventeen other places fell into his hands without a struggle. He then resolved upon the conquest of Júnagarh. This was a renowned fort in the country of Súrath, and was held by the grandsons of Amín Khán. Former rulers had been able to make no impression upon it. On the 23rd Khurdád, his army reached the vicinity, and seventeen batteries were raised round the lofty fortress. Núr Beg Khán and some others were detached to check the *Káthis*, who were rendering assistance to the besieged. A great fire broke out in the fortress, causing much destruction; and the European artillery officer, who had embraced the Muhammadan religion, fell dead into the fosse. This greatly encouraged the assailants. But the garrison had abundant supplies, and were confident in the strength of the place. They had a hundred guns, some of which discharged balls of one *man* and a half, and these they fired several times daily. Khán-i 'Azam at length placed some mortars on an eminence commanding the fortress, and opened fire upon it. This disturbed the confidence of the garrison, and a capitulation was proposed. The siege had lasted three months, but the keys were given up on the 7th Shahryúr. In all, fifty-seven persons of distinction surrendered, all of whom were honourably treated, and received honorary dresses and *jágírs*.

THIRTY-EIGHTH YEAR OF THE REIGN.

Preparations for the Invasion of the Dakhin.

[Text, vol. iii. p. 683.] The expostulations and advice addressed to Burhánu-l Mulk made no impression upon him, so the Emperor resolved to proceed to Ágra to organize a force for service in the Dakhin. On the 25th Mihr, Prince Dániyál was directed to march thitherwards. Khán-khánán, Rái Singh, and many other nobles, with treasure, artillery, and elephants, were ordered to accompany him. Sháh Rukh Mirzá, Sháhbáz Khán, and other chiefs of Málwa, were ordered to join with their forces. Rájá Mán Singh was also directed to march from Bengal, if that province could be safely left. Prince Sultán Murád was instructed to prepare to take part in the campaign. * * At the town of Shaikhupúr, Khán-khánán was summoned to an audience, and he then represented that the most favourable time for an invasion of the Dakhin was after the end of the rains, when grain and fodder might be procured in abundance. So Prince Dániyál was recalled, and the Emperor resolved to head the expedition himself at the conclusion of the rains. * * Khán-khánán was directed to proceed to Ágra, there to collect and organize the forces, and the Emperor returned homewards.

FORTIETH YEAR OF THE REIGN.

War between Ahmadnagar and Bíjápúr.

[Text, vol. iii. p. 713.] Since the time when the Emperor withdrew his gracious attention from the Dakhin, fresh misfortunes had fallen upon that country, and discontent grew rife. Nizámu-l Mulk Burhán was dead, and his son Ibráhím, who succeeded him, took to evil courses. An army marched from

Bíjápúr against him, and on the 16th Amurdád a battle was fought about forty miles from Ahmadnagar, in which he was killed by an arrow. The Bíjápúr army returned triumphant, and the Nizámu-l Mulkí forces were scattered abroad.

Invasion of the Dakhin.

[Text, vol. iii. p. 741.] Prince [Murád], in pursuance of orders, now prepared for the invasion of the Dakhin; but Khán-khánán was delayed by the tardy gathering of his men. Before he joined, some little dissension had sprung up between them. The Prince's desire was that the heads of the army should all join him, and proceed by that road [from Gujarát] to the Dakhin. It was the opinion of the commander-in-chief (Khán-khánán), that he should advance from Málwa. As their opinions did not agree, the Prince, on the 20th Ábán, marched from Ahmadábád, and rested awhile at Broach, in expectation of getting more men. On the 22nd Khurdád, he left Broach. Khán-khánán remained for some time at Bhílsa, which was in his *iktá'*, to assemble his forces. On the 9th Amurdád, he marched for Ujjain. This greatly incensed the Prince, who sent him an angry message. He wrote in reply that he would join the Prince's army as soon as he had received the promised contingent from the ruler (*marzbán*) of Khándesh; the Prince might meanwhile enjoy the pleasures of the chase in Gujarát. The Prince was enraged with this reply, and his flatterers fanned his anger. He marched with his army towards Ahmadnagar.

The chief nobles, and Rájá 'Alí Khán, were inclined to the Prince, and when Khán-khánán became aware of this, he left his army, artillery, and elephants with Mirzá Sháh Rukh and other *amírs*, while he started off express with Rájá 'Alí Khán (to meet the Prince). On the 19th Ázur, he met the Prince at the fort of Chánd, thirty *kos* from Ahmadnagar. The meeting was not cordial. After a great deal of talk, a *darbár* was held. When the army moved, there was no unity of feeling. Khán-khánán, with his numerous force, was offended, and kept aloof from the management of the business. Sádik Khán brought up an old grievance which he had against Sháhbáz Khán, and rarely went to the *darbár*. On the 8th De, the army encamped half a *kos* from the city, and on that day Khán-khánán and Sháhbáz Khán went to the city (*ba shahr raftand*). Through their negligence an attack was made upon the baggage of the army, which was with difficulty repelled, and the people of the city were encouraged by the evident signs of dissension. On the 8th, the fortress was invested. Chánd Bíbí, sister of Burhán, prepared for resistance. As they had carried off Ahmad,[1] the son, Ikhlás Khán came to Ahmadnagar with Motí, and being defeated, fled to Pattan.

When the royal army approached, Manjúh (the *wazír*) carried off Ahmad, with a portion of the treasure and some of the elephants, to Bíjápúr; but he was nearly taken prisoner. From want of proper munitions, the siege was protracted. Chánd Bíbí was afraid of being taken prisoner; but being informed of the condition of the assailants, she was encouraged to defend the city. On the 9th, Sháh 'Alí and Abhang Khán made a night attack in force upon the battery of Khán-khánán; but the defenders fought bravely, killed many of the assailants, and repelled the attack. If the repulse had been followed up, the pursuers might have entered the fort with the fugitives, and the place would have fallen.

The close blockade and scarcity of provisions were taking effect on the garrison. * * On the 13th, an unsuccessful attack was made upon the camp. * * On the 16th, a caravan from Gujarát came near, and was plundered by Sa'ádat Khán. * * On the 19th, Sher Khwája, Shaikh Daulat, Kámrán Beg, and Daulat Khán, were sent with a force towards Pattan. They inflicted a defeat on Ikhlás Khán, and secured great booty. Then, eager for further plunder, they pillaged the inhabitants of

[1] Ahmad Sháh, who claimed to be of royal descent, had been raised to the throne. An opposite faction had set up Motí, a bázár boy, and he having been taken prisoner Ikhlás Khán procured another child, who was also called Motí.—Briggs, Firishta, vol. ii. p. 270; vol. iii. pp. 291, 292.

Pattan, a city which had received letters of protection. On the 11th Isfandármuz, a portion of the wall was broken down. A mine was carried from the battery of the Prince, and a hole cleared out under the wall. It was filled with powder and exploded, when it brought down about thirty *gaz* of the wall. The troops were ready for the assault; but another mine, which had been carried under the wall from the battery of Sháhbáz Khán, was discovered by the garrison and emptied. From fear of a disaster like that which occurred at Chítor, the storming party was held back, and such a delay occurred, that the daylight passed away, and during the night the garrison repaired the breach. But the garrison was greatly disheartened by the activity of the besiegers, and now proposed an accommodation. They offered to elevate Bahádur, son of the son of Burhánu-l Mulk, to the throne, with the title of Nizámu-l Mulk, and as a vassal of the Imperial throne. The territory of Ahmadnagar was to be confirmed to him, and the province of Birár given up to the Emperor. Jewels, the pick of the elephants, and other things were to be sent as tribute to the Emperor. Notwithstanding the desperate state of the place, and the scarcity of provisions, these unworthy terms were agreed to, and a treaty was concluded on the 17th Isfandármuz.

Forty-first Year of the Reign.

Famine.

[Text, vol. iii. p. 744.] In this year there was little rain, and the price of rice rose high. Celestial influences were unpropitious, and those learned in the stars announced dearth and scarcity. The kind-hearted Emperor sent experienced officers in every direction, to supply food every day to the poor and destitute. So, under the Imperial orders, the necessitous received daily assistance to their satisfaction, and every class of the indigent was entrusted to the care of those who were able to care for them.

Defeat of the Dakhin Confederates.

[Text, vol. iii. p. 764.] The Ahmadnagar affair, and other unfortunate matters, had brought disgrace upon the armies of the Dakhin, and made their leaders desirous of retrieving their fortunes, by contending against the Imperial forces. Sháh Murád was at the head of the royal army, and was desirous of giving battle, but the experienced *amirs* objected, and continued their opposition, until Mirzá Sháh Rukh was appointed commander-in-chief, and Khán-khánán and other distinguished officers were named for different duties. The military chest, the elephants, and the artillery, were carefully looked after, and everything properly arranged. Mirzá Sháh Rukh and Khán-khánán commanded the centre. * * The army marched from Sháhpúr, and took up a position twelve *kos* from Pathari.

The enemy also prepared for battle. The army of Nizámu-l Mulk was in the centre; the 'Ádil Khánís were on the right, and the army of Kutbu-l Mulk on the left. On the 28th Bahman, after the first watch of the day, the river Gang (Godávarí) was passed, and the battle began by an attack on the right wing of the enemy. But they held their ground firmly in a strong position, and kept up a heavy fire. Great bravery was exhibited on both sides, and a long and desperate struggle was maintained. The enemy was numerous, and the superiority of his fire checked the Imperial ranks and made them waver. Jagganáth and several other Rájpúts drew rein, and did not move, while the 'Ádil Khání troops made an onslaught upon Rájá 'Alí Khán of Khándesh. He made a stubborn resistance, and fell fighting bravely, with thirty-five distinguished officers and 500 devoted followers.

Mirzá Sháh Rukh and Khán-khánán had been successful in their part of the field, so also had Saiyid Kásim and other leaders. The enemy was under the impression that the ruler of Khándesh was in the centre, and thought that Mirzá Sháh Rukh and Khán-khánán were involved in his defeat. During the darkness of the night, the opposing forces remained separate from each other, each supposing that it had gained a victory. In the course of the night many of the scattered troops rejoined their standards. Under the impression that Rájá 'Alí Khán, of Khándesh, had gone over to the enemy, the Imperial troops plundered his baggage. Dwárka Das of the advance, and Sa'íd Jalál of the left, retired to Nílawí. Ram Chandar, who had fought bravely, and had received twenty wounds with the forces under Rájá 'Alí Khán, remained among the wounded during the night, and died a few days after.

When morning came, the Imperial forces, 7000 in number, found themselves in face of 25,000 of the enemy. They had all night suffered from thirst, and they now carried the river Sugám. The enemy was only half-hearted, and being dismayed by this demonstration took to flight, and made but little resistance. * * Worn out by the protracted conflict, the Imperial forces were unable to pursue. At the beginning of the campaign, the Imperial forces numbered only 15,000, while the enemy were 60,000 in number. Still they had gained this great victory, and had captured forty elephants and much artillery.

Forty-third Year of the Reign.

Abú-l Fazl sent to the Dakhin.

[Text, vol. iii. p. 802.] On His Majesty's return from the Panjáb, he formed the design of marching direct to the south without visiting his capital. But his mind was disturbed by the non-arrival of the Princes, and many idle stories were reported to him. So he halted, resolving to make a politic delay, and he again summoned the Princes to his presence. On the 25th of the month, the author of this work received orders to proceed to the Dakhin, and to bring Prince Sultán Murád to Court. If the *amírs* of the Dakhin were willing to undertake the management of the country, the author was to leave it in their hands, and return with the Prince; but if otherwise, he was to send the Prince to Court, and to remain and associate himself with the other officers in supporting Mirzá Sháh Rukh. A banner and kettle-drums were given to the Mirzá, and the province of Málwa was assigned to him, so that he might be able to raise and equip an army in his own province, and return to the Dakhin when called upon.

Daulatábád.

[Text, vol. iii. p. 803.] At the beginning of Isfandármuz, the fort of Lohgarh, at Daulatábád in the Dakhin, was taken. Mirzá 'Alí Beg Akbarsháhí besieged it for a month, and want of provisions and water compelled the garrison to surrender and give up the keys.

FORTY-FOURTH YEAR OF THE REIGN.

Kherla and Násik.

[Text, vol. iii. p. 805.] In this year the fort of Kherla, in Birár, lying between Birár and Gondwána, was obtained by capitulation on the 13th Ábán, the garrison being short of provisions. The fort of Násik, near Ahmadnagar, was taken soon after.

Death of Prince Sultán Murád.

[Text, vol. iii. p. 806.] Alas, that wine should be burdened with suffering, and that its sweet nectar should be a deadly poison! * * On the 17th Urdibihisht, near Dihbárí, on the banks of the Púrtá, twenty *kos* from Daulatábád, Prince Sultán Murád's fits took a grave character, and on the 22nd he became insensible and died.

FORTY-FIFTH YEAR OF THE REIGN.

Ásír.

[Text, vol. iii. p. 837.] On the 22nd Isfandármuz, Khán-i 'Azam, Ásaf Khán, Shaikh Faríd, and the writer of this work were directed to invest the fortress of Ásír, and to construct batteries round it. But the force which was sent on this service, under the command of Shaikh Faríd, was very small compared with the numbers of the enemy; so it was deemed prudent to halt at three *kos* from the fortress. Some inexperienced and mischievous persons excited the Emperor's anger at this resolution. But the writer went to visit him, and explained the true state of affairs, and his anger was soon appeased. On the same day the author was appointed to take charge of the province of Khándesh. Thereupon he established twenty-two stations in the province, and to each he appointed a responsible officer. To one he appointed his brother Shaikh Abú-l Barakát, with some experienced subordinate officers; to another his son Shaikh 'Abdu-r Rahmán. In a short time the refractory were brought to obedience, and many others gladly became subjects of the Emperor. The soldiery submitted peacefully, and the peasantry applied themselves to the work of cultivation.

Bengal.

[Text, vol. iii. p. 828.] Disturbances now broke out in the province of Bengal, through the imprudence of Rájá Mán Singh, who, although he was absent in the province of Ajmír, kept the government of Bengal in his own hands, thinking that all would go on quietly, and according to his wish. 'Usmán, Shujáwal, and other Afgháns, broke out in rebellion. Mahá Singh and Partáb Singh made light of this, and attacked them at Bhadrak; but were defeated. The province was not lost; but the rebels got possession of some places.

Disobedience of Prince Salím.

[Text, vol. iii. p. 831.] Salím, the Prince Royal, had been sent against the Ráná (of U'dípúr). His love of ease, encouraged by his improper companions, induced him to spend some time at Ajmír in pleasure. After a while, he hastened to U'dípúr, and the Ráná then leading his forces in another direction, plundered Bálpúr and other places. Madho Singh was sent against him, and defeated him. But before this honourable service was accomplished, the Prince was induced by his evil counsellors to form the design of going to the Panjáb, and of there following his own pleasure. But just at this time came the outbreak of the Afgháns in Bengal, and upon the advice of Rájá Mán Singh, he proceeded thither. On the 1st Amurdád, he crossed the Jumna, four *kos* from Ágra, and greatly pained Maryam Makání, the Emperor's mother, by not going to see her. In her kindness she went out after him, to chide him for his neglect; but when he heard of her approach on his return from hunting, he entered his boat, and went off as fast as he could, leaving the venerable lady to return home with sorrowful heart. The Prince went on to Allahábád, where he seized upon many *jágírs*. He appropriated the revenues of Bihár, amounting to more than thirty *lacs* of rupees, and assumed the royal title. The Emperor, in his kindness and forbearance, did not believe all this, and his great nobles agreed with him. Letters were sent to the Prince questioning him upon his irregular proceedings, and he replied that he was doing good service, and was innocent of any wrong.

Ahmadnagar.

[Text, vol. iii. p. 832.] The operations against Ahmadnagar were protracted, and the royal army was in difficulty about supplies. Evil-disposed persons in all parts began to move. So, on the 4th of the month, Mirzá Rustam was sent to Prince (Dániyál) with a *lac* of *mohurs*. Násik fell into the hands of the Imperial officers about this time.

After the rains the Emperor set his heart upon the reduction of Ahmadnagar. He sent directions for using every effort, and he himself proceeded to Burhánpúr. Chánd Bíbí was for keeping the treaty which she had made with the writer of this work; but Abhang,[1] at the head of a large force of Abyssinians and Dakhinís, was fighting against her. On the 26th Farwardín, the royal army arrived, and suspicion seized upon the Dakhiní

[1] The Nihang Khán of Briggs.

forces. One man whispered to another that their leaders had made terms with the Imperial army; so this force of Abhang's lost heart, and dispersed without making any resistance. On the 2nd Urdibihisht, the various intrenchments were assigned to the various *amírs*. Chánd Bíbí was for abiding by the treaty. Several of the leading men in the fortress then took matters into their own hands, and made several unsuccessful sorties. Under the direction of the Prince, great efforts were made to form a *khák-rez*[1] to fill up the ditch and reach to the walls. This was from thirty to forty *gaz* broad, and seven *gaz* deep (*sharfá*). The wall was of bluish stone, and twenty-seven *gaz* high. Mines were formed from the trenches of the Prince and Mirzá Yúsuf Khán; but the besieged broke into them, and filled them up again. They even formed a counter-mine from the inside, and exploded it; but it was smothered by the *khák-rez* and did no damage there. The shock split a bastion of the fortress. When this was discovered, efforts were made to clear out the chasm, and this being effected, 180 *mans* of gunpowder were placed therein. On the 6th Shahryúr, it was exploded. The bastion and thirty *gaz* of the wall was blown into the air. The garrison suffered from the falling stones; but not a particle of stone fell on the besiegers. Through the breach rushed the assailants, and another party made their way in from the intrenchments of Mirzá Yúsuf Khán. Fifteen hundred of the garrison were put to the sword; the rest were saved by the solicitations of their friends. Bahádur, son of Ibráhím and grandson of Burhán, who had been set up as Nizámu-l Mulk, was taken prisoner. Very valuable jewels, embossed arms, a splendid library, fine silks, and twenty-five elephants, were among the booty. The guns and ammunition exceeded all compute. The siege was carried on during the rainy season; but by great good fortune there was no flooding to interrupt

[1] Johnson explains this as "the foot of a wall," but the words mean literally "earth-spreading," and the text makes it clear that it signifies the filling in of the ditch, and the levelling up of dirt against the walls.

the construction of the *khák-rez*. The day after the victory, heavy rain commenced. The siege lasted four months and four days.

Death of Jalála the Sectary.[1]

[Text, vol. iii. p. 835.] A party of Lohánís who had come to Ghazní upon business had been attacked from an ambush by the Hazáras. After seven days' fighting, they were compelled by thirst to retire, and they then sought the aid of Jalála. He went with them into Ghazní, in the disguise of a merchant. When they were attacked by the men of Sharíf Khán, and by the *raiyats*, Jalála tried to get them back again to their homes. Again the Hazáras fell upon them and scattered them abroad. Jalála was wounded and carried to the hills, where he was put to death by Murád Beg and other intelligent men.

Disturbances in the Dakhin.

[Text, vol. iii. p. 844.] Although Ahmadnagar had fallen to the Imperial arms, a scarcity of grain soon after weakened their power; the malcontents again assembled, and broke out in rebellion. They placed at their head 'Alí, son of Sháh 'Alí, and uncle of Murtazá Nizámu-l Mulk. Khán-khánán was therefore appointed to take command at Ahmadnagar, and the writer of this history was sent to Násik.

Forty-sixth Year of the Reign.

[Text, vol. iii. p. 849.] The writer of this history was held back from going to Násik, and marched against the son of Sháh 'Alí, which was deemed to be more important. In Isfandármuz in the preceding year, he had joined Khán-khánán, near Barangánw. But intelligence was brought that one of the great vassals of 'Ádil Khán Bíjápúrí was coming towards Ahmadnagar with

[1] Jalála is generally called *tárikí*, "sectary." Chalmers, in his MS. translation, read the word as "*Tájik*," and, strange to say, Elphinstone has adopted that word in one of his notes. Jalála's followers, as Elphinstone shows, were Yúsufzáis, not Tájiks.

5000 horse and 12,000 foot. The Khán deemed it necessary to watch his proceedings, so he proceeded to Jálna-púr, and left the author to march against the son of Sháh 'Alí. On the 27th, the author reached the banks of the Ganga (Godávarí). On the 29th he got possession of the fort of Kálna, which is one of the chief fortresses of Ahmadnagar. * * 'Alí Mardán Khán, the commander of the Imperial forces, was defeated and taken prisoner in Telingána.

The author's efforts were thereupon directed to the repression of this outbreak, and he sent his son with 1200 horse against the enemy. * * On the 6th Khurdád, he defeated them with a loss of 400 killed, and many wounded.

TAKMÍLA-I AKBAR-NÁMA

OF

INÁYATU-LLA.

THIS is the supplement of the *Akbar-náma*, containing the four remaining years of Akbar's reign. It was composed by Shaikh Ináyatu-lla, and is sometimes met with bound up with the *Akbar-náma*.

[The above is all that has been found among Sir H. M. Elliot's papers concerning this "Completion of the *Akbar-náma*." There is no copy of the work in his library, and not a page of translation. The work seems to be almost unknown in England, for it is not to be found in the Libraries of the British Museum, the East India Office, or the Royal Asiatic Society. A translation of the whole work is given at the end of the MS. translation of the *Akbar-náma* belonging to the Royal Asiatic Society, already noticed at p. 8 *suprà*. It is the work of "Lieut." Chalmers, of the Madras Army, and was used by Elphinstone. The following Extracts are taken from this translation, and may be accepted as accurate.

Nothing more has been learnt of the work or its author than what he tells us in the following pages. It will be seen from the conclusion that he calls himself "Ináyatu-lla, or Muhammad Sálih."]

EXTRACTS.

The most admirable command of His Most High Majesty * * was issued to this effect, that as the *Akbar-náma* was still unfinished, and Abú-l Fazl was no more, and had not attained the happiness of completing this noble record, this humble individual (Ináyatu-lla) should relate the annals of four years which remained unchronicled. And as the second volume of the Shaikh was both deficient in beauty of style, and contained many obsolete words unintelligible to the generality of mankind, a point which was not approved of, he was further directed to arrange his diction and phraseology after the model of the first volume, so that his meaning, though wonderful and sublime, should be clad in the familiar garb of common language, and that it might thus be understood and commended by small and great. My hope is, that by obedience to this mandate, the morning of success and complacency may dawn upon me, and that I may thus secure an ample stock of approbation and advancement!

Forty-seventh Year of the Reign.

This year commenced on Thursday, the 27th Ramazán. * * About this time, a letter arrived from the Prince Sultán Dániyál, reporting that (Malik) Ambar had collected his troops in Bidar, and had gained a victory over a party which had been sent to oppose him by Malik Baríd. After exacting tribute from him, Malik Ambar successfully attacked the Kutbu-l Mulkí territories, and then proceeding towards Telingána, had besieged Mír Murtazá in Pathrí. The Prince, therefore, to prevent his junction with the son of Sháh 'Alí in Ahmadnagar, had detached the Khán-khánán against him, while Shaikh Abú-l Fazl was ordered against Ráju.

Prince Salím.

It has already been related, that His Highness the Prince Sultán Salím had set out against the Rájá of Ajmír, attended by a train of followers countless as the stars. But as Akbar had now heard of the disturbances in Bengal, he had countermanded the Prince, and directed him to unite his forces with those of Rájá Mán Singh, to reduce these Eastern rebels, and that the Prince deferred his departure, and merely hunted towards Allahábád..

When the Emperor was at Akbarábád (Ágra), the Prince wrote to request the honour of an audience, and proceeded as far as Etáwa for the purpose; but here doubts were suggested to him by some ill-inclined persons, and he feared to advance any further. His Majesty was no sooner made aware of this circumstance, than he wrote to the Prince, that "if he were earnest in his wish to pay his respects, he ought to display his confidence by doing so alone, and dismiss his attendants to their *jágírs;* if, on the contrary, suspicion withheld him, he had better retire to Allahábád, there to re-assure his heart, and repair to Court when he was able to do so with full trust and confidence." The Prince, alarmed at this kind yet disdainful communication, instantly despatched *Mír Sadr-i Jahán*, who was the chief justiciary of the Imperial dominions, and His Majesty's agent with the Prince, to his august father, charged with the most submissive apology, and referring to the Mír's own observation in testimony of his sense of duty and allegiance. He then set out towards Allahábád, and meanwhile an Imperial *farmán* was issued, investing him with the government of Bengal and Orissa, and directing him to despatch his officers to take possession of those two provinces. Rájá Mán Singh was, at the same time, ordered to transfer the provinces, and to return to Court.

Defeat of Malik Ambar.

A splendid victory was gained by the Khán-khánán over Ambar. It had been reported by Mír Murtazá and Sher Khwája, that Ambar had been joined by Farhád with 2000 horse, and had strengthened himself in Nandeir. The Khán determined to send his own son, Mirzá Írich, with a body of brave followers, against him. As fate had ordained the day of punishment for Ambar to approach, he was sufficiently bold to draw out his forces, and prepare for battle in the vicinity of Nandeir. Mirzá Írich, chafing at his insolence, marshalled his brave forces and attacked him. The centre and left soon bore down their opponents, and if the right had in like manner gained the same honourable title to fame, it is most probable that the whole of the enemy would have been taken, and the sedition quelled at once. Even as it was, twenty elephants, with all the enemy's equipage, were taken.

Afgháns in Bengal.

'Usmán the Afghán trod in the path of rebellion, and crossing the Brahmaputra river, was in vain opposed by Báz Bahádur, the Imperial *thánadár*, who retired to Bhowál. Rájá Mán Singh no sooner heard of Báz Bahádur's retreat, than, marching the whole night, he joined him on the following morning, and attacking the enemy put him to flight, and took many guns and much spoil. The Rájá having then again delivered the country to Báz Bahádur, returned to Dacca; but as the officer of the district now formed the idea of crossing the river and seizing upon the country of 'Ísá, and Sarípúr and Bakrampúr, the Afgháns again assumed a posture of defiance, and defended the approaches both with guns and boats. As the contest continued for some time, the Rájá sent a chosen body in advance, with orders to cross the river when they could get the opportunity. But the Afgháns opened a discharge of artillery upon them from their boats, and many of the warriors were killed. The Rájá now opportunely arrived in person, and with his men boldly crossing the river on elephants, the enemy, astonished at their daring, took to flight. The Rájá drew not his rein till he had followed them to Tíra and Mahwarí. Then Ghazní, the chief of the latter place, submitted, and the Rájá pushed on. He took Bakrampúr and Sarípúr, and stationed trusty forces throughout the country. The Afgháns then retreated to Sunárgánw, while the Rájá returned victorious to Dacca.

Death of Shaikh Abú-l Fazl.

As Shaikh Abú-l Fazl adorned the garment of the high consideration in which he was held with the embroidery of hearty fidelity, he had reported to His Majesty some of the youthful indiscretions of the Prince Salím Mirzá, the heir-apparent—forgetful that the high road to honour and distinction hath its dangers, and that the branch which wildly ventures to run crookedly must ever bear bitter fruit.

To His Majesty's amiable disposition, therefore, his reports were not entirely acceptable, and, as this soon became current among all classes, Akbar summoned him to Court, and directed him to make over his retinue and command during his absence to his son 'Abdu-r Rahmán. Abú-l Fazl reached Sarái Banga,[1] two stages from Gwálior, on the 1st Shahryúr. There Bar Singh Deo Bundela, anxious to obtain the favour of the Prince Sultán Salím, planted an ambuscade in his way. Abú-l Fazl's followers apprised him of the danger, and recommended him to retire for protection to Rái Ráyán and Rájá Rái Singh, who were with 2000 horse at Antarí, a distance of only two *kos*. But the Shaikh, whose hour of death was at hand, and the gem of whose discrimination had therefore grown dull, only replied, "The fear of death is vain, for its period cannot be deferred. I have been raised by my gallantry from the position of being son of a *darwesh* to the rank of nobility, how then shall I basely seek shelter from another?" The Rájpúts soon afterwards placed their rough hands upon his collar, and slew him with his attendants. His head was sent by Bar Singh Deo to the young Prince. His Majesty was much affected on hearing of his death, and he earnestly besought pardon for his sins from the Creator. Orders were issued for bringing Bar Singh Deo to punishment.

Prince Dániyál.

Prince Dániyál, with the levity of youth, had forgotten the vow which he had made by the head of his august father to

[1] According to Asad Beg, who had personal knowledge of the matter, the place of the murder was called "Sarái-Barár," and the murderer's name was Nar Singh. See *infrá*,—*Wikáya'-i Asad Beg.*

forsake the habit of drinking, and had again addicted himself to wine. Akbar addressed to him a letter of exhortation, bidding him take warning by the fate of Prince Sultán Murád, and entreating him, if only out of regard to his earthly parent, to withdraw his hand from the impurity of this venomous and treacherous poison.

Prince Salím.

The Sultána Salíma Begam took her departure for Allahábád, in order that she might by her influence bring to the Imperial Court the Prince Sultán Salím, who had been repeatedly reported to have thrown the veil of repentance over his offences. He was therefore pressingly and graciously invited to the presence.

Bar Singh Deo.

Bar Singh Deo, the murderer of Abú-l Fazl, had first been pursued by the Rái Ráyán to Bhánder, and from thence to I'rich, a strong fort on the river. When the advanced party of the Imperial troops turned their conquering face against this place, he came out and drew up his troops to dispute the bank of the stream.[1] The Rái Ráyán crossed and attacked, and drove him back again into the fort, which was then besieged by the royal forces. The distress of the enemy increased, till the benighted culprit broke from the walls by night, and fled to the jungle. His elephant was slain there; but he contrived, under the darkness of the night, to effect his escape.

Forty-eighth Year of the Reign.

Reconciliation of Prince Salím.

The Sultána Salíma Begam, having interceded between His Majesty and the young prince Salím, reconciled the monarch to the wonted exercise of paternal affection, while at the same time she also procured for Salím the pardon of Akbar's august

[1] The Betwa.

mother. When the Prince approached the capital, that venerable matron proceeded some days' journey to meet him, and brought him to her own private abode. Even His Majesty, to conciliate his illustrious son, advanced several steps to receive him. * * After a short interval, His Majesty conferred on him the royal diadem, which is the main source of ornament to the Court and Sovereignty, and the chief light of the pomp of royalty.

Defeat of the Magh Rájá.

This short-sighted Rájá, who had just now acquired the country of Bangu, and secured possession of the gold hoarded for many years, became elated with the extent of his treasures and the number of his elephants. He had succeeded by his wiles in bringing over Kaid Rái, the *zamíndár* of Bakrampúr, who had been forcibly reduced by Mán Singh. He then openly rebelled, and assembling an army at Sunárgánw, laid siege to a fort in the vicinity. Sultán Kulí Khán the governor bravely defended himself, and eventually sallying forth, dispersed the besiegers. Ahmad, another rebel, then joined the Rájá with his forces, and a second time summoned Sultán Kulí. Rájá Mán Singh, hearing of the increased numbers of the enemy, despatched a force under Ibráhím Atka, Raghu Dás, and Dalpat Rái, to his assistance. These soon brought the Magh Rájá and all his forces to action, for as victory ever attends the Imperial standards, they attacked him, regardless of the number of his boats and the strength of his artillery. A complete victory was gained. One hundred vessels, of different kinds, were taken; and the Rájá was compelled to intrench himself in front of the Imperial troops, to provide safety against their attacks.

Rájá of Bánswárra.

About the same period the Rájá of Bánswárra, who had excited a rebellion, was defeated by Mirzá Sháh Rukh, whose admirable zeal called him to the field, notwithstanding the infirm state of his health. The Rájá was defeated after a short contest; his stronghold was taken, and himself driven to the hills. He next raised a party in Málwa, and the Mirzá, thinking it more important to repress him than to seize his territory, promptly followed him thither. On this, the rebel immediately returned, and re-occupying his own country, increased in insolence. The roads were impassable in consequence of the rains, and the Mirzá, being unable to move his troops, was compelled for the present to suspend the pursuit.

Prince Salím.

His Majesty had already once deputed Prince Salím to uproot the rebellious Ráná, and the standards of victory had already overshadowed U'dípúr. Another force had also been sent to reduce the hill-country. But the Ráná escaped to his fastnesses, and the consummation of this important affair was delayed. An order was now again issued that the Prince should a second time brace his courage to the destruction of this doomed infidel. * * But the inclinations of the young Prince were not heartily engaged in the enterprise. He reported that his troops were not prepared, and made extravagant demands, both for increased forces and treasure. Moreover, he intimated his wish, that if his exorbitant requests were not complied with, he might be allowed to return to his own *jágír*. His Majesty, accordingly, guessing the object of his conduct, directed that he might consider himself at liberty to return to Allahábád, and to present himself at Court whenever afterwards he chose to do so. The Prince accepted this permission, and marching on the 6th A'zur, crossed the Jumna, near Muttra, and turned towards Allahábád.

Bíjápúr.

Shortly after, the irrevocable commands were issued to Prince Sultán Dániyál and the Khán-khánán to march against 'A'dil Khán of Bíjápúr, who was dilatory in the transmission of his tribute, and had otherwise shown himself refractory. * * The young Prince was ill, and unable to proceed himself; but by the advice of his counsellors, he deputed Ináyatu-lla to Bíjápúr, with a despatch calculated to excite both the hopes and fears of 'Ádil Khán.

Kaid Ráí of Bengal.

Rájá Mán Singh, after defeating the Magh Rájá, turned his attention toward Kaid Ráí of Bengal, who had collected nearly 500 vessels of war, and had laid siege to Kilmak, the Imperial commander in Srinagar. Kilmak held out, till a body of troops was sent to his aid by the Rájá. These finally overcame the enemy, and after a furious cannonade, took Kaid Ráí prisoner, who died of his wounds soon after he was brought before the Rájá.

Almshouses and Saráis.

At this period almshouses were directed to be established throughout the Imperial dominions; also caravanserais for travellers at every stage, where food was to be prepared and held in readiness at all times for the way-worn traveller, who is usually too fatigued to be equal to the exertion of cooking his own repast.

Imprisonment of the Emperor's Nephew.

Prince Kaikubád, son of Mirzá Hakím, having contracted the pernicious habit of indulging in intoxicating drugs, was sent into confinement in the fort of Rantambhor, under the custody of Rájá Jagannáth, there to be kept until punishment and seclusion from corrupt society should work in him amendment.

Forty-ninth Year of the Reign.

Bíjápúr.

'Ádil Khán of Bíjápúr, being now wrought on by the exhortations of Mirzá Sharfu-d dín, the Imperial ambassador, to offer his allegiance to the State, Mirzá Írich was the noble honoured with the charge of extorting both the tribute which he agreed to send, and the litter of his daughter, who was to be united to Prince Sultán Dániyál. That young prince was also prevailed on to proceed with 5000 horse to Ahmadnagar, to celebrate the rejoicings on the occasion of the nuptials.

Rájá Mán Singh's Sister.

The death of the sister of Rájá Mán Singh, who was the chief favourite in the harem of the Prince Sultán Salím, occurred at this time. This lady was ever ambitious of an ascendency over the other inmates of the harem, and grew violent at the slightest opposition to her will. Having one day had a quarrel with one of her rivals, she took the opportunity of the Prince's absence at a hunting party, to swallow a large quantity of opium; preferring, in her fury, the draught of deadly poison to the sweet waters of life. She expired before the Prince, who was recalled from his excursion by the news of her illness, could arrive, and he remained for some days absorbed in grief for her loss.

Prince Dániyál.

It now became necessary to despatch to the Court of Sultán Dániyál Shaikh Abú-l Khair, brother of Abú-l Fazl, and equally devoted with that chief to the service of the Emperor, to endeavour by any means to bring the young Prince to Court, with the view there to force him to abstain from the ruinous course of inebriety which had now reduced him to the most debilitated condition.

Prince Salím.

Reports arrived that the practice of indulgence in wine drinking, and of the excessive use of opium, had affected the health of the Prince Royal, Sultán Salím, and had made his temper so irritable and tyrannical, that the slightest offences were visited with the severest punishments, that pardon was never thought of, and that his adherents were struck dumb with terror. His Majesty, aware that a word of counsel spoken in season, would avail more than a thousand at a distance, * * determined to proceed to Allahábád, to attempt the reformation of the Prince.

Death of the Emperor's Mother.

[The progress of the Emperor to Allahábád] was arrested by the accounts which he received of the dangerous illness of his august mother, and his affectionate heart was overwhelmed with grief at her distressing state. * * On the 20th Shahryúr she departed, leaving the world in grief. Akbar clad himself in the deepest mourning, shaved his head and beard, and avoided all ornament in his apparel. Her body was conveyed to Dehlí. His Majesty himself placed his shoulder under the bier, and helped to bear it for several paces, and the same office was performed by the chief *amírs* of the State. Her remains were interred near to those of her illustrious husband.

The Murderer of Abú-l Fazl.

The abode of Bar Singh Deo, the murderer of Abú-l Fazl, had been several times attacked and plundered, but the culprit himself had still escaped the vengeful pursuit of Shaikh 'Abdu-r Rahmán. Orders were now given for the reinforcement of that officer with as many of the Imperial troops as he might select as worthy, from their valour and conduct, to be partners in the work of retribution. Rájá Bikramájít was also associated with him.

Fiftieth Year of the Reign.

Capture of Urcha.

Shaikh 'Abdu-r Rahmán and Khwája 'Abdu-lla reported that they had succeeded in taking the fort of Urcha,[1] one of the strongest in Hindústán, and that the rebel, Bar Singh Deo, had

[1] Eight miles from Jhánsí.

been driven to hide himself like a snake among the wilds, to escape the pursuit of the Imperial warriors. Shortly afterwards another despatch was received from the same chiefs, stating that as the enemy had poisoned all the wells, and 1000 men had died of fever, they had been compelled to abandon Urcha as a place of residence.

Death of Prince Dániyál.

Shall I talk of the changeableness of this world, or shall I relate the sad tale of this young branch of tender years, or shall I rather acquaint my pen with the evil which his own obstinacy and folly wrought upon himself! The fire of the wine-cup extinguished the light of his natural abilities, and the lamp of his intellect was unable to burn through the abundance of this baneful liquid. The affectionate arguments of His Majesty were disregarded, till by degrees the fumes of wine sapped the strength and vigour of his constitution, and his trembling limbs lost their functions. The Khán-khánán and Khwája Abú-l Hasan used their utmost endeavours, both in obedience to the Imperial orders and the real affection they felt for him, to stop the supply of this deleterious liquor. They posted guards to prevent its introduction; but the base parasites who were about the Prince's person contrived to introduce the poison unperceived, sometimes concealing it in the barrels of muskets, and sometimes in their turbans. After forty days of illness, the young Prince died, at the age of thirty-three—an event which caused both friends and strangers to sit down in grief and mourning.

Bar Singh Deo.

It has been already related that Bar Singh Deo took refuge in the wilds and forests. He was, nevertheless, pursued by Rájá Jai Singh, who shot many of his followers, and at last wounded the blood-stained murderer, who, however, still contrived, though with blistered feet, to effect his escape.

Death of the Emperor.

On Monday, the 12th Ábán, corresponding with the 20th Jumáda-l awwal, 1014 Hijra (September, 1605), an illness insinuated itself into the frame of the Emperor, and he became indisposed. Hakím 'Alí, who was the most skilful of physicians, was summoned to attend. After considering the symptoms, he refrained for eight days from administering medicine, under the hope that His Majesty's vigour of constitution would overcome the disease. On the ninth day, the debility and symptoms appeared to be aggravated, so the physician resorted to the remedies of his art; but they produced no good effect for ten days. The complaint in the bowels increased, and the limbs lost their power. It then became evident that recovery was hopeless, and that the collar of the world was in the clutches of the Fates.

On the 9th Ázur, corresponding with the night of Wednesday, 12th Jumáda-l ákhir (13th October, 1605 A.D.), when the age of His Majesty had reached the period of sixty-five lunar years, he bade adieu to life, in the capital of Ágra, and took his departure to the paradise of love. On the following day his sacred remains were borne by men of all ranks, in stately and becoming pomp, to the grave, and were interred in the garden of Bihishtábád.

Conclusion.

Praise be to God, that this excellent work, the *Akbar-náma*, has been brought to an admirable and approved conclusion! * * The second volume, up to the forty-seventh year of the reign, is the composition of the most learned and intelligent Abú-l Fazl, son of Shaikh Mubárak; and from the forty-eighth year, after the death of the celebrated Shaikh, Ináyatu-lla or Muhammad Sálih, after duly preparing himself for the work of history, has thus brought it to an end.

AKBAR-NÁMA

OF

SHAIKH ILLAHDÁD, FAIZÍ SIRHINDÍ.

[OF this writer very little is known, except what we gather from the work before us. His father was Mullá 'Alí Sher, a learned man, among whose pupils was Nizámu-d dín Ahmad, the author of the *Tabakát-i Akbari*. Shaikh Illahdád was a native of Sirhind, and held a *madad-ma'ásh* village in that district. He was attached to the service of Shaikh Faríd Bokhárí, who held the office of *Bakhshíu-l Mulk*, and he seems to have accompanied that nobleman on his various services. He tells us that it was by the express command of Shaikh Faríd that this history was written. He began it in the thirty-sixth year of his age, having up to that time "been greatly devoted to social pleasures and delights." This same Shaikh Faríd was also patron of another historian, Shaikh Núru-l Hakk, whose work, the *Zubdatu-t Tawáríkh*, will be noticed soon after this.

The *Akbar-náma* of Shaikh Illahdád is a plain unambitious work, and has no pretensions to originality. It is based on the *Tabakát-i Akbari*; but the author sometimes prefers the narrative of Abú-l Fazl, and adapts that writer's florid and somewhat prolix descriptions to his sober and straightforward style. Thus the accounts of the murder of Atka Khán and the conquest of Garha-katanka are taken from Abú-l Fazl. On one subject only does he enter into more particular details—the services rendered by his patron, Shaikh Faríd Bokhárí. With this exception, and the addition of scraps of poetry and some wonderful stories, the work is nothing more than a compilation from the *Tabakát-i Akbari* and the *Akbar-náma* of Abú-l Fazl. It ends with the latter work in 1010 H. (1602 A.D.).

The author claims to have taken part in the compilation of the "*Humáyún Sháhi*[1] of Mihtar Jauhar," and upon the Emperor Akbar being informed of this fact, he expressed his approval, and his intention of employing him to turn some Hindí work into Persian.

A few Extracts have been translated. The first one by Ensign F. Mackenzie, the remainder by the Editor.

Sir H. Elliot's copy of the *Akbar-náma* is an octavo volume of 453 pages, 15 lines to a page.]

EXTRACTS.

An Account of the manner in which the Khwája 'Abdú-l Majíd A'saf Khán conquered the country of Panna[2] *and Garha-katanka, by the eternal good fortune of His Majesty.*

It is not unknown to those who are acquainted with the events of this period, that Khwája 'Abdú-l Majíd Harawí was originally a scribe, who had, during the reign of the late blessed monarch, been constantly employed in transacting the affairs of the household. During His Majesty's fortunate reign, he had also held similar offices of trust. Step by step he obtained promotion, and received the title of A'saf Khán. A *jágír* was given him in the *sarkár* of Garha-katanka, which is a very spacious country. Katanka is a separate village near Garha. In the year 970, and the eighth year of the reign, his experience induced him to desire to gain possession of the land of Panna, which adjoined his own possessions. He sent an urgent message to Rájá Rám Chand, whose ancestors had always ruled that country, and with whom Ghází Khán Tátár had taken refuge after his flight from the Court of the Asylum of the Universe. He counselled him strongly for his own welfare to become a subject of His Majesty, and pay him tribute. He also recommended him to send Ghází Khán, who had been a rebel, and received shelter from him, to the Protector of the World.

Ram Chand's ill-fortune and pride prevented him from being moved by these representations, and he made preparations for war. Ásaf Khán, being free from apprehension, and trusting in the eternal success of His Majesty's arms, brought an army against him. Rájá Rám Chand, aided by Ghází Khán Tátár, and a vast multitude, like locusts and ants, also drew up in battle array. Both parties did their best, and fought valiantly; but, at last, Rám Chand was routed, and Ghází Khán and many others were put to the sword. Rájá Rám Chand fled thence to the castle of Mándhún, which is noted for being one of the strongest fortified places in Hindústán. Much plunder fell into the hands of the victorious troops. Shortly afterwards Rájá Rám Chand, repenting of what he had done, by the assistance of several of the chief Rájás who were faithful subjects of the King, was admitted into the train of the submissive and obedient. A royal *farmán* was despatched to the effect, that as Rájá Rám Chand had taken the best course for his own good, and submitted himself, his country was not to be invaded. On the receipt of this order, Ásaf Khán returned to his own *jágír*, and took measures for the reduction of Garha, which was near his own territory.

[1] The chief place of that country is Chaurágarh. The land contains 70,000 inhabited villages. It is bounded on one side by Málwa and the Dakhin, on another by Garha. It is a separate principality, governed by a Rání named Durgávatí, who was remarkable for her beauty and loveliness. Ásaf Khán, whose possessions her country bordered on, and whose people were constantly going to and fro, managed to make himself well acquainted with its general condition, and the state of its revenues. He began to ravage and plunder the villages in its districts, waiting for an opportunity of taking more extreme measures. At last, in the year 971, in the ninth year of the reign, he valiantly set out with 10,000 horse and foot, purposing to take possession of the country. His valour made him look

[1] [See *suprà*, p. 30.]

on this as a matter of easy accomplishment. The Rání, owing to her pride and confidence in her own skill and courage, attended to her own affairs, and utterly disregarded the fact that she had a neighbour whose valour had been proved on several occasions, particularly in the case of Báz Bahádur, who had attacked him with the Afgháns of the tribe of Míyánah, and whom he had vanquished. She had always kept up a force of 20,000 horsemen, but she was suddenly told that the valiant troops of His Majesty had arrived at Damúda, one of her chief towns, at a time when her troops were dispersed. She had only 500 men with her. Adhár, who was entrusted with the management of the whole business of that country, informed her how affairs stood. The Rání said, "This is through your stupidity. I have long ruled this country, and never acted in such a manner as to bring disgrace on myself. Now, from what you tell me, if the King were here in person, I would present myself before him; but now there is no remedy but war!" The Rání made four marches from that place, and found herself face to face with the Imperial army.

A'saf Khán had gone as far as Damúda with great speed, but he delayed there. The Rání thus had time to collect some 4000 men, and her courtiers recommended her to give battle, advising her, however, to post herself in some strong position until the arrival of more troops. The Rání agreed to this counsel, and retreated into the jungles and strong places, so that A'saf Khán became ignorant of her whereabouts. A'saf Khán turned back from that place, and on reaching Garha, he took possession of its villages and territories. In the mean time, 5000 men had been collected. When A'saf Khán was informed of the Rání's movements, he left a force in Garha, and proceeded in person against her. The Rání was informed of this, and said to her people, "How long shall we take refuge among the trees and jungles?" She then made up her mind to fight, and mounting her elephant, she went amidst her troops, endeavouring by suitable exhortations to encourage and prepare them for war. When both armies met, a desperate battle began. Three hundred Mughals obtained martyrdom, and the Ráni pursued the fugitives.

At the close of day, the Ráni consulted with her chiefs as to what was best to be done, and every one said something. The Ráni was of opinion that she had better return to her camp, and thence make a night attack, or else remain where they were until daybreak and then renew the battle, because, in the event of her not doing something, Ásaf Khán would seize the hill in the morning, and post his artillery on it. Having determined on a night attack, she returned to her camp, but no one agreed with her on this matter, or showed any resolution. At daybreak, what she had predicted, happened. Ásaf Khán possessed himself of the summit of the hill, and having fortified it, he took post there with his army. The Ráni again, intent on fighting, drew up her soldiers and mounted her best elephant. She caused Adhár, who has been mentioned before, to ride before her on her elephant. Such a conflict took place, that, throwing away guns and arrows, the combatants seized each other's collars, and fought hand to hand.

Rájá Bírsáh, the heir-apparent, behaved with the utmost valour. The conflict lasted until the third watch of the day, and the Rájá repulsed the royal troops three times, but at last he was wounded. When the Ráni learnt what had happened to her son, she directed her confidential servants to convey him in the best way they could from the field of battle to a place of safety, which they did. Whilst this was going on, so large a body of men went away from the Ráni, that not more than 300 remained with her. Notwithstanding this, she firmly maintained her ground, and encouraged her men to fight. Suddenly fate directed an arrow, which struck her on the temple. This she courageously drew out herself, but its barb remained in the wound. This arrow was followed by another, which wounded her in the neck, which she extracted in the same way, but fainted from excess of pain. When she came round, she said to Adhár, who was in front of her, "I have always placed trust and confidence in you against a day like this; so that, in the event of my meeting with defeat, you might not suffer me to fall into the hands of the enemy. Adhár had not the power to do what she required, so she drew out her dagger, and died a manly death. Very many of her confidential adherents loyally gave up their lives. By the favour of the Almighty, and the fortune of the King of Kings, a victory, the splendour of which exceeded all other victories, was obtained. A thousand elephants, and countless booty, fell into the hands of the victorious troops, and an extensive territory was added to His Majesty's dominions.

A'saf Khán, after the lapse of two months, proceeded towards Chaurágarh. The Rání's son, who had gone thither from the field of battle, came out to oppose him; but after a short struggle, the army of the King gained possession of the fort. In it were found a great amount of gold, priceless jewels, gold and silver plate, and images of their divinities, together with other valuables and property, which had been collected there by the Rájás during many centuries, as is the custom of those people. All these fell into the hands of A'saf Khán; a hundred and one cooking pots, full of large and valuable gold coins, came into his possession. The performance of this notable action caused his pomp and dignity greatly to increase, and men placed great trust in him. Nevertheless, this faithless man only sent 200 out of the 1000 elephants which he had captured as a *pesh-kash* to Court, and withheld the jewels and valuables altogether. His Majesty's magnanimity overlooked this, and he took no notice of the circumstance. A'saf Khán remained established in the government of Garha and Karra, until His Majesty proceeded to Jaunpúr for the purpose of chastising Khán-zamán.

* * * * * * *

A most remarkable event occurred at Chaurágarh. When Rájá Bírsáh, the Rání's son, was shut up there, a certain number of men were appointed, in the event of a defeat, for the purpose of performing the *jauhar*, an ancient custom of the Rájás of

Hind. On occasions like this, they shut their women up in the house, and after heaping up straw, wood, cotton, and ghee around it, they set fire to the pile and burn them. This they look upon as a means of saving their honour. When the fort was nearly reduced, they did this, and all the beautiful women were reduced to ashes. After the capture of the place, when the flames had ceased on the second day, they examined the place, and discovered two females underneath a large block of wood. One of them was the Rání's sister, the other the Rájá's wife, with whom he had not yet cohabited. They were taken out unhurt, and sent to the royal harem.

The Mirzás.[1]

[The Mirzás were the sons of Muhammad Sultán Mirzá. He was the son of Rashíd Sultán Waís Mirzá, son of Bábakrá, son of Mansúr, son of Bábakrá, son of 'Umr Shaikh, son of Sáhib Kirán Amír Tímúr. The mother of Sultán Mirzá was a daughter of Sultán Husain Mirzá, ruler of Khurásán. This Sultán (Husain) Mirzá brought up his grandson, Muhammad Sultán Mirzá, under his own protection. When Sultán Mirzá died, dissensions arose in his country, and Muhammad Sultán Mirzá went and presented himself to the Emperor Bábar, who treated him with great kindness. After the death of Bábar, the Emperor Humáyún kept up during his reign the same favour and patronage. Muhammad Sultán Mirzá had two sons. One, Ulugh Mirzá, met his death in a fight with the Hazáras. The other was named Sháh Mirzá. Ulugh Mirzá left two sons, Sikandar Mirzá and Muhammad Sultán Mirzá. Upon the death of Ulugh Mirzá, the Emperor Humáyún charged himself with the education of his sons, and by his favour Sikandar Mirzá received the title of Ulugh Mirzá, and Muhammad Sultán

[1] [Nearly the whole of this Extract is taken from different parts of the *Tabakát-i Akbarí*, but it is here given entire as being the most connected account of these Mirzás, troublesome in their own time, and perplexing to posterity.]

Mirzá that of Sháh Mirzá. When the Emperor Akbar succeeded to the throne, Muhammad Sultán Mirzá had grown up. The Emperor exempted him from military service, and assigned him the *pargana* of 'Azampúr, in the *sarkár* of Sambal, for a maintenance. He had several sons. First, Ibráhím Husain Mirzá; second, Muhammad Husain Mirzá; third, Mas'úd Husain Mirzá; fourth, 'Ákil Husain Mirzá. The Emperor conferred upon each of these a suitable *jágír*, and raised them to the rank of nobility. They attended in the train of His Majesty, and performed the duties of service. When the Emperor returned from his campaign against Jaunpúr, they were at their *jágírs* in Sambal. At the time of the Emperor's march to Lahore against Mirzá Hakím, the brothers Ulugh Mirzá and Sháh Mirzá combined with their uncles (nephews?) Ibráhím Husain Mirzá and Muhammad Husain Mirzá, and breaking out into rebellion, ravaged several *parganas*. This was an old failing in the family. Ulugh Mirzá and Sháh Mirzá, sons of Muhammad Sultán Mirzá, rose in rebellion during the reign of Humáyún, and did great damage. But on each occasion their offences were overlooked.

When these graceless men attacked the *parganas*, the *jágírdárs* of those parts resisted them, and the Mirzás, being unable to withstand the force brought against them, made off to join Khán-zamán and Sikandar Khán. There also their intractable tempers stood in the way of anything like union, so they turned back, with the intention of making an inroad into the Doáb, and went as far as the *pargana* of Ním-kahár. Here Yár Sháhí, the sister's son of Hájí Khán Sístání, *jágírdár* of that district, gave them battle; but although he made a good fight, he was defeated, and great booty fell into the hands of the Mirzás. They continued their course, plundering as far as Dehlí. Tátár Khán, the governor of Dehlí, put the fort in a state of defence, and Mun'im Khán moved up from Ágra to oppose them. Unable to resist the forces brought against them, they hastened off to Málwa, which was in a defenceless state. At the town of

Sonpat, they fell in with Mír Mu'ízzu-l Mulk, who was proceeding to the Panjáb, and plundered his baggage. They then proceeded to Málwa, and took possession of that country. Kadam Khán, brother of Maghrib Khán Dakhiní, was in Hindia, and Muhammad Husain Mirzá laid siege to the place. After a time, he killed Kadam Khán, and got possession of Hindia. When intelligence of these doings reached the Emperor at Lahore, he gave orders for arresting Muhammad Sultán Mirzá at 'Azampúr, and for keeping him a prisoner in the fort of Bayána.

In this same year, 947 H., the Emperor having proved victorious over 'Alí Kulí Khán-zamán and Bahádur Khán, returned to Ágra, and his victorious army had hardly taken breath, when the news came of the descent of the Mirzás upon Málwa. The Emperor immediately went off thither. When he reached Gágrún, he did not deem it necessary to prosecute a design which might as well be carried out by his officers; so he appointed Shahábu-d dín Ahmad Khán, Sháh Bidágh Khán, and some others, to act in the province of Mandú. As these nobles came near to Ujjain, they learned that the Mirzás, having heard of the approach of the Emperor, had met together and gone off to Changíz Khán, the ruler of Gujarát. So these commanders, by the grace of God, and the good fortune of the Emperor, obtained possession of the province without opposition or fighting.

In the year 975, when the Emperor had sent his forces to besiege the fort of Rantambhor, he received intelligence that the Mirzás had fled from Changíz Khán, and having come back into Málwa, had laid siege to Ujjain. So he sent against them Kalij Khán and some other *amirs* who had been named for service at Rantambhor. When these *amirs* approached Sironj, they were joined by Shahábu-d dín Ahmad Khán, the governor of that *sarkár*, and Sháh Bidágh Khán, governor of Sárangpúr. The Mirzás hearing of this imposing force, raised the siege of Ujjain, and turned towards Mandú. The garrison being thus relieved, came out, and having joined the army, the united forces went in pursuit of the rebels. They fled from Mandú to the Nerbadda, and lost many men in making the passage of that river. Just about this time, Jhajár Khán Habshí assassinated Changíz Khán, the ruler of Gujarát, in the *tirpauliya*. When the Mirzás were informed of this event, they thought the disturbances in Gujarát opened a favourable field for them, so they proceeded thither, and the Imperial *amírs* returned to their *jágírs* or to Court, according to orders. The Mirzás, having obtained possession of Chámpánír, marched against Broach, and laid siege to the fortress. After a time, they killed by treachery Rúmí Khán, who held the fort, and each of them brought a portion of the territories of Gujarát into his possession. Ibráhím Husain held Baroda and the surrounding territories. Muhammad Husain got Surát and its dependencies, and Sháh Mirzá held Chámpánír, with its dependent districts.[1]]

Campaign in the Siwálik.

[Armaments had been several times sent under different *amírs* of distinction to effect the subjugation of Jammú, Rámgarh, and other places; but this difficult enterprise had never been satisfactorily accomplished. So, on the 10th Muharram, 1003, the Emperor sent Shaikh Faríd *Bakhshíu-l Mulk*, with several other *amírs* and a considerable force, to effect the conquest. He had great confidence in the ability and resolution of the *Bakhshí*. The force marched to the Siwálik hills, and the *Bakhshí* resolved to begin by attacking Jammú, one of the strongest forts in that country, which had once been reduced after considerable resistance by Salím Khán Súr. The Rájá made signs of resistance, and it was resolved to attack him before the army proceeded to occupy the territories of the rebels in other directions. Husain Beg and some other officers were accordingly sent against him. When the Rájá and the *zamíndárs* heard of the approach of the

Imperial forces, they were greatly alarmed, and surrendered the fort of Jammú. After placing a garrison in the place, the *Bakhshi* marched against the fort of Rámgarh, which he took by assault, and placed in the custody of the men of Nawáb Zain Khán Koka. Husain Beg now returned and joined the main force.

Another force was now sent under Páyinda Kákshál, to receive the submission of such Rájás and *samíndárs* as were willing to pay their allegiance, and to coerce those who resisted. The army then proceeded towards Jasrúná and Lakhanpúr, and the Rájás and *samíndárs*, who had long been independent, submitted and paid their revenue. On reaching Sámba, Bhabú, the Rájá of Jasrúná, and Balídar, the *samíndár* of Lakhanpúr, came in. This Bhabú had been the leader of the rebels, and the great promoter of the strife. * * Next day Súraj Singh, son of Bású, the Rájá of Mú, came in, and made his allegiance, and he was placed in charge of Husain Beg Shaikh 'Umarí, until it should be determined by the Emperor how the *parganas* of Sámba and Jasrúná should be disposed of. Two *kos* from Sámba a fort was built. Muhammad Khán Turkomán was sent forward to take charge of Lakhanpúr.

The army next proceeded to the village of Aliya, where Bhabú was, and there encamped. This is a strong place, surrounded on all sides by jungle so dense, that it was difficult to pass through it. Hither the rebels and fugitives fled and hid, deeming themselves safe from all pursuit. Shaikh Faríd stayed for some days at that village, and gave orders for clearing away the jungle by the axe and by fire. The soldiers were engaged in the work for several days; but were unable to clear away more than a road of twenty or thirty *gaz* wide. Several of the old trees which were fit for building purposes were cut down and sent to Lahore for use in the government buildings. Bhabú, before mentioned, had been the chief and most active of the rebels, and he had done an immense deal of harm. A royal order had been given, that no effort should be spared to capture him. Now that he was in the hands of the army, it was determined to send him to the Emperor in charge of 'Alí Muhammad.

When the army reached Jasrúná, the native place of Bhabú, his sons and brethren and friends gathered together, and took up a strong position at a small castle on a hill. This hill was covered with jungle from top to bottom, with only one narrow way, along which one or two horsemen might pass. On each side of this road there was a wall, with loopholes through which muskets might be fired, and arrows shot, upon strangers and foes, to prevent their approach. At the bottom of the hill, on the level ground, there was a cultivated tract, in which there was a fort, with moats. Shaikh Faríd, when he perceived these hostile preparations, determined to capture the place, and punish the rebels. He first sent forward Husain Beg to attack the lower fort. By great exertion the moat was filled, the gates burst open, and the fort was taken. Several of the assailants were killed by wounds from gun-shots and arrows. Then the troops entered the jungle to attack the upper fort. The enemy hotly disputed the passage through the jungle with their muskets and bows. But the valiant soldiers returned the fire, and pressed on till they reached the gate of the fort. Then they set fire to the place, and the rebels fled for refuge into the jungle. All the buildings and crops were burnt.

Husain Beg halted here, and sent intelligence of his success to Shaikh Faríd. An answer was returned, directing him to fortify the place and stay there the night, or to leave a detachment, and himself rejoin the main force. It was late in the day, the army was two *kos* distant, the way through the jungle was narrow and difficult, and the returning force might be attacked at great disadvantage; so Husain Beg resolved to rest for the night, and to make his way back in the morning. All night long the enemy harassed them from all parts of the jungle with arrows; but according to the plan agreed upon, each man sat behind his breastwork (*morchal*) with his shield over his head, never moving or making a noise. The night was thus passed mid a constant rain of arrows; but in the morning the forces made their way through the jungle, and effected their junction safely. Husain Beg obtained great praise for his gallantry, and rewards in *in'áms*, money, and robes were bestowed upon the officers and soldiers.

Having left Husain Beg there with a garrison, the army proceeded towards Lakhanpúr. The Rájá came out to meet it. The *pargana* was given to Muhammad Khán Turkomán, and a sufficient garrison was placed in the fort. Then the army crossed the Rávi by a ford, and proceeded to the *pargana* of Pathán; next day it marched to Mú, a *pargana* under the authority of Bású. At this time Bású was at Court, but his son had at the first come forward and accompanied the army. He was now told that he ought to seize the opportunity for sending a suitable offering in acknowledgment of the country having been graciously confirmed to him. The son of Bású sent two *vakíls* to invite the *Bakhshí* to his home, a fort on the top of a hill, to receive the tribute. So the chief men of the army proceeded with an escort to Mú, which is a very strong fort. Excepting some cultivated land immediately joining the fort, the whole hill is covered with impenetrable jungle. The road through is very narrow, and in places strong gates are erected across it. At the foot of the hill there is also cultivated land, and around it there are stone walls and deep ditches. The country round is exceedingly pleasant, the gardens are full of fruit trees, and there are plenty of running streams. Bású's residence was a fine extensive building. The place was visited and examined, and after Bású's *vakíls* had discharged the duties of hospitality, the tribute was brought forth, consisting of valuable horses and fine cloths. The other territories of the neighbourhood, which had been held by rebellious Rájás and *zamíndárs*, were granted to *jágírdárs* as *tankhwáh*.

The army then proceeded to Gwálior, which is also a strong fort belonging to a different Rájá, who came out to meet the army and show his loyalty. The Rání of Nagarkot, whose son was at the Imperial Court, sent her *vakíl* to pay her respects. On every side the rebels were compelled to submit, and show their obedience. All the country which had been in the hands of the rebels between Jammú and Nagarkot was reduced, and the Rájás and *zamíndárs* made their submission, or received merited punishment. In fact, the country was subjugated in a manner which it had never been before.

The affairs of the clan (*jamá'at*) of the Jasuwálas, who are *zamíndárs* with a (common) army, now had to be settled. But when they heard of the approach of the royal army, and of the reduction of the territories of the *zamíndárs*, all hope of successful resistance was beaten out of them, and they made humble submission.

Intelligence now arrived that Kází Hasan had been appointed to relieve Shaikh Faríd. The reason of this was, that the Emperor greatly valued the services of the Shaikh, and when he learned that the country had been reduced, and there remained but little to require his presence there, he appointed Kází Hasan, who had formerly seen service and gained experience in the hills under the son of Kalij Khán, to go and relieve the Shaikh, and to finish what yet remained to be done in concert with the other nobles in the army. Shaikh Faríd Bakhshí was to return to Court. When the Kází arrived, the *Bakhshí* represented that there still remained some work to be done, and it seemed advisable for him to remain a few days and accomplish his work, after which he would proceed to Court. It might be that things which were easy for him might become difficult after his departure. But the Kází did not assent to this, and urged immediate submission to the royal command. So, at the beginning of the month of De, the *Bakhshí* started, and travelling express by way of Desoha and Batála, he reached Lahore in three days, and having paid his respects to the Emperor, received great honours.

About this time Khwája Nizámu-d dín Ahmad Bakhshí, the author of the *Tabakát-i Akbar-sháhí*, died, being nearly forty-eight years of age, on the 22nd Safar, 1003 H., and the thirty-ninth year of the reign.

On the 22nd Rabí'u-l ákhir, Nawáb-i 'Azam Khán returned from Mecca, and was graciously received by His Majesty. His son, Mirzá 'Abdú-lla, was with him, and he also received many marks of the royal favour. * * On the 27th of the month Koka died at Lahore. On the 3rd Rabí'u-s sání Ásaf Khán, who had been sent to Kashmír, having performed his mission, returned to Court. He accomplished the journey from Kashmír in three days. At the end of Jumáda-s sání, despatches arrived announcing the taking of the fort of Síwí after an arduous siege. Many of the defenders were slain, and great spoil was secured. Mír Ma'súm Bhakkarí,[1] one of the bravest men in the army, had taken a distinguished part in the siege, and was richly rewarded.

THIRTY-NINTH YEAR OF THE REIGN.

The thirty-ninth year began on the 9th Rajab, and was celebrated as usual. * *

At this time Muzaffar Husain, ruler of Kandahár, who had submitted to the authority of the Imperial throne, wrote to say that he would surrender Kandahár to any one whom the Emperor might appoint. Sháh Beg Khán Kábulí had been ordered to proceed thither. He had not yet reached the place; but in the month of Sha'bán intelligence was brought of his arrival there, and of Muzaffar Husain having delivered the place into his hands. Muzaffar then repaired with all his family and followers to the Imperial Court, having received as a present from Sháh Beg 20,000 rupees in cash, 600 camels, several elephants, and a great supply of different kinds of tents. When he was at four *kos* distance from Lahore, the Emperor sent Bakhshí Shaikh Faríd to meet him, and in the month of

[1] The author of the *Táríkh-i Ma'súmí*.—See Vol. I. p. 212.

Zí-l hijja * * he received him, and appointed a suitable place for his abode. (*Banquets given and offerings made at the Nau-roz.*)

In the month of Safar the Emperor went to pay a visit to Shaikh Faizí, who was on his death-bed. Soon after he got back to the palace word was brought that the Shaikh was dead. Shaikh Faizí was a man of great talents, and fond of the society of the learned. In his early days he and the author of this work had some connexion through using the same *takhallus* for their writings. * * *

On the 15th Zí-l ka'da the King went out on a stag hunt. A stag made a rush upon him, and wounded him in the thigh with his horns. There was no one close by to save him, so he was knocked down. Men then came and caught the stag. The Emperor had received a severe wound. It was closed up by the surgeons; but after a few days it swelled and gave him such great pain that he was obliged to keep to his couch for several days: in the end it came all well, and his recovery was celebrated with great rejoicings. * * *

Victories in the Dakhin.

(*Suprà*, p. 95.)

There are three distinct States in the Dakhin. The Nizámu-l Mulkiya, 'Ádil Khániya, and Kutbu-l Mulkiya. The settled rule among them was, that if a foreign army entered their country, they united their forces and fought, notwithstanding the dissensions and quarrels they had among themselves. It was also the rule, that when their forces were united, Nizámu-l Mulk commanded the centre, 'Ádil Khán the right, and Kutbu-l Mulk the left. This rule was now observed, and an immense force had been collected. Some severe fighting had gone on, and the enemy had lost nearly 1000 men, who fell fighting bravely. On the Imperial side, also, Rájá 'Alí Khán, ruler of Ásír and Burhánpúr, who had accompanied the army, was slain. Ram Chandar Kachhwáha was wounded, and lay a whole night among the dead, and plunderers cut off his ears, for the sake of the pearls which he wore in them. In the first day's action, fighting went on from mid-day to the third hour of evening, when the enemy fell back to his camp. In the evening and morning of the next day Khán-khánán put his army in motion against the enemy, and when he approached, the enemy came out boldly to meet him, and the battle began. A fierce elephant rushed from the enemy's line, and charging upon the Imperial array, the elephants turned and fled before him. He then charged the line of soldiers; but they made a way for him to pass through. After he passed right through the line, Khán-khánán delivered his attack upon the enemy. In a short time he beat back a large body of them with considerable slaughter, made many prisoners, and gained a complete victory.

[*Great fire at the royal palace.—Account of the Emperor's journey to Kashmír, with description of Srinagar and other places.*]

On the 29th Rabí'u-s sání, 1006, Prince Rustam, son of Prince Sháh Murád, died in the tenth year of his age. His mother was sister of Khán-i 'Azam.

On the 5th Rajab died 'Abdu-lla Khán Uzbek, ruler of the whole of Máwaráu-n nahr, Turkistán, Badakhshán, a great part of Khurásán, Sístán, Ghor, Ghorjistán, etc. He was a bold courageous ruler, and no other descendant of Changíz Khán had such an extensive dominion. He reigned forty-two years. * *

On the 13th Sha'bán, the new year [43] of the Iláhí began.

Death of Ma'súm Kábulí.

At this time (Zí-l hijja, 1007), intelligence arrived of the death of Ma'súm Kábulí, and only a few days afterwards the death was reported of 'Ysá Khán, a chief of Bengal, with whom he had taken refuge.

Conquest of the Dakhin.

The Emperor Akbar had subjected to his rule the whole wide expanse of Hindústán, with the exception of a portion of the

Dakhin, the rulers of which had, nevertheless, sent in former years representatives and presents to the Imperial throne. But some of these rulers had since failed in duly discharging their obligations, and had thus wounded the pride of the Emperor. Prince Sháh Murád, Khán-khánán, and other *amírs* had been sent to effect the conquest of the country. The Prince went to that country, and distinguished himself by his services. Other *amírs* were afterwards sent, who fought bravely, and subjugated a considerable portion of the country. The work of conquest was still progressing, when it entered the heart of Prince Salím[1] that he would proceed thither to support the *amírs*, and to accomplish the reduction of the remainder of the country, so that diversities of religion might be swept away, and that the whole country might repose in peace under the Imperial rule. For five or six years the conquest had been retarded by the bickerings of the *amírs*, and so he resolved to proceed from Lahore to the Imperial presence at Ágra, there to obtain information of the true state of affairs, because that place was nearer to the scene of action; and after due consultation, to proceed thither in person should it seem necessary.

When intelligence arrived of the death of Prince Sháh Murád, Prince Dániyál was sent thither; but the Emperor not feeling at ease upon the state of affairs in the Dakhin, resolved to proceed in that direction, by making a hunting excursion to Málwa. His intention was to send a strong reinforcement to Prince Dániyál, under Bahádur, son of Rájá 'Alí of Khándesh, and to rest awhile in Málwa till events took a favourable turn. The Emperor accordingly left Ágra, * * and on the 21st of the month, after showing great honour and favour to Khán-khánán, he sent him on in advance. * * On the 7th Rabí'u-s sání, the Emperor reached Dholpúr. The river Chambal was crossed by fords, and His Majesty went over on an elephant. On the 17th he reached the fort of Gwálior. * * * On the 29th Jumáda-s sání, he passed through Sironj, and on the 1st Rajab

[1] He is already called by his subsequent regal name "Sháh Jahángír."

the royal camp was pitched between Káliyáda and Ujjain. This city Ujjain is one of the most ancient in Hindústán, and contains many relics of antiquity. Káliyáda is the name of one of the most delightful places in the world. * * Here the Emperor rested for awhile, expecting that Bahádur Khán, son of Rájá 'Alí Khán of Khándesh, would come to wait upon him.

Rájá 'Alí of Khándesh had been slain fighting bravely under Khán-khánán against the Dakhinís, and it was expected that his son would now come forward to give his services to the Imperial army, in the hope of revenging his father's fall, and of gaining the Imperial favour. Even while the Emperor was encamped at Ujjain, some intimation was received about his intentions, and he now sent an envoy to the Emperor, charged with many excuses and foolish evasions. Hereupon His Majesty, in his great kindness, sent Mírán *Sadr-i Jahán,* to Khándesh, to ascertain the exact state of affairs, and to remove any doubts which might have crept into the mind of Bahádur Khán.

The ambassador proceeded to Khándesh, and ascertained that when Bahádur Khán succeeded Rájá 'Alí Khán, he was a prisoner in the fort of Ásír. For it was the established custom among the rulers of Khándesh, that the reigning potentate kept his sons, brothers, and other relations in confinement, to guard against attempts upon the throne; so these unhappy persons, with their wives and families, passed all their lives in confinement. Bahádur Khán had passed nearly thirty years in prison, and knew nothing whatever of the ways of the world, and the business of government. When he came out of prison, and the title of ruler devolved upon him, he plunged recklessly into dissipation. No trace of the tact and nobility which had distinguished Rájá 'Alí Khán was to be found in him. Unmindful of his obligations and obedience to the Imperial throne, he showed no gratitude and sent no tribute; nor did his craven spirit entertain one thought of avenging his father. When this became known to the Emperor, he remembered the loyalty and devotion of the late Rájá, and sent Mírán *Sadr-i Jahán* to give good counsel to the young Prince.

Mírán proceeded to Ásír. Bahádur Khán received him at first with great respect and honour, and acknowledged the allegiance and duty he owed to the Emperor. The envoy on his side gave him good counsel and advice, and endeavoured to excite in him a spirit of loyalty. But fate was against the young ruler; he paid but little heed to good counsel, and persisted in his own perverse conduct. Sometimes he said he would go to see the Emperor; at others, that suspicions had been aroused in his mind by people's talk, which would not allow him to make this visit at present; but he promised to send his son with suitable offerings, if the Emperor would graciously direct him to do so. After awhile, when all the dependents of the Imperial throne should have been confirmed in their places, and he should be able to throw off his feeling of shame, he would proceed in person to pay his respects to the Emperor. These excuses proceeded either from his wavering disposition, or from a settled design to act treacherously. When Mírán, the envoy, found that his representations had no effect upon Bahádur, he communicated the result to the Emperor. This roused great anger in the breast of the Emperor, and was the cause of his sending Shaikh Faríd Bokhárí to Khándesh.

On the 14th Sha'bán, while the Imperial camp was at Dhár, Shaikh Faríd *Bakhshiu-l Mulk* received orders to lead a considerable force against the fort of Ásír. His instructions were to re-assure and advise Bahádur Khán. If he proved tractable, he was to be brought to the presence of the Emperor; if not, the *Bakhshi* was to invest the fort of Ásír, and reduce it with all possible speed. The Imperial officers were eager to proceed on this service, partly out of zeal in the service of the Emperor, partly from the wish to serve under the *Bakhshi*. Among those who accompanied him were * * and a large number whose names are too numerous to recount.

With this select force, the *Bahhshi* crossed the Nerbadda, and sought to get information about the enemy. He then learned that the forces of Bahádur Khán were under the command of Sádát Khán, son-in-law of the late Rájá 'Alí Khán, the greatest and the most trusted of all his servants. He had been sent towards Sultánpúr and Nandurbár, to make a diversion against the Imperial forces in that quarter. It was resolved to detach a force to watch this party, while the remainder marched through Khándesh. On arriving at Gharkol, a humble and submissive letter was brought from Bahádur Khán, recounting the services of his ancestors, and offering to send his son with suitable offerings to the Emperor. He also made excuses for his conduct, and solicited the kind intercession of Shaikh Faríd to avert the consequences of his faults. The Shaikh sent this letter to the Emperor, and waited for an answer. The Emperor sent a gracious reply, offering to forgive his transgressions and to receive him into favour if he would hasten to pay his allegiance.

Marching forwards, the army passed over the summit of Sabalgarh, and arrived on the confines of Khándesh. Mírán *Sadr-i Jahán* had previously advised that the force should be sent to Burhánpúr, lest its advance upon Ásír should drive Bahádur Khán to desperation. But when this opinion was represented to the Emperor, he the same day gave orders that no attention was to be paid to it; that the army was not to go to Burhánpúr, but was to march direct to Ásír, and invest the place. Accordingly, it advanced to within two or three *kos* of Ásír.

On arriving there, it was learned that Mírán *Sadr-i Jahán* and Peshrau Khán, who had also been sent by the Emperor to Bahádur, after alternately trying persuasion and menace, were unable to make any impression upon him, and had retired from Ásír to Burhánpúr. From thence they reported the failure of their mission, and left the Emperor to determine what was best to be done. On the 21st Sha'bán the Emperor proceeded to Mandú. [*Description of buildings.*] When Shaikh Fáríd came near to Ásír, Bahádur Khán sent him another letter, containing the same appeals for merciful consideration, and offering the same excuses as he had made before. In reply, he was reminded how the kings of the Dakhin had united their armies, and had made war upon the Emperor's allies, and how Rájá 'Alí had fallen fighting bravely and loyally upon the Imperial side. The Emperor was now resolved upon revenging his death, and, with God's help, would annex the territories of all the three kings to the Imperial dominions. His duty, therefore, was to join the army with his followers without delay, and to take revenge for his father's blood—not to be a thorn in the way, and to say to the Emperor, "First strike me, and then the murderers of my father." But fortune had turned her back upon the family, and the graceless fellow would listen to no reason or expostulation.

The rulers of Khándesh were of the Fárúkí tribe, and the family had held rule in the country for more than 200 years. An ancestor who had connexions with the Dakhin, and had served there as a soldier, being aggrieved, left that country and went to Khándesh, which country was then held by different *samíndárs* and Rájás. He came to a village which pleased him, and there a dog which accompanied him set off in pursuit of a hare, but the hare turned round and attacked the dog. This unusual exhibition of courage greatly impressed him, and he thought that the land where such a sight could be seen must be fertile in courage and daring, so he resolved to take up his abode there. He expressed his wish to the *samíndár* of the place, but it was refused. Afterwards he seized an opportunity of seeking assistance from the King of Dehlí, and having collected some of his brethren (tribesmen?), he overpowered that *samíndár*, and took possession of the village. He extended his power over other villages around, and in the end he was master of several *parganas*, and commander of an armed force.

When he died, his authority descended to his grandson, who saw the value that a fortress would be as a place of safety for his family and dependents. Ásír, which is situated on the top of a hill, was at that time an inhabited place. He contrived by various stratagems to obtain this place from the *samíndár* who held it, and fortified it strongly. He then assumed the name of ruler, and at length the whole country of Khándesh, about 150 *kos* in length, and 50 in breadth, more or less, came under his sway. These rulers acted so wisely and carefully that the kings of Dehlí did not interfere with them. * * Upon the Government descending to Rájá 'Alí Khán, he showed himself to be a man of great administrative powers, and it is probable that no one of the dynasty had been his equal in intelligence and ability. People of neighbouring and distant countries had been induced by his just and generous rule to take up their abode in his country. Among the best proofs of his intelligence was his loyalty to the Imperial throne, his obedience, and the magnificence of his offerings, in all which he excelled the other princes of the region.

His successor, Bahádur Khán, had none of his ability, and advice was thrown away upon him. The line was drawing to a close, and fortune had averted her face. Shaikh Faríd invested the fort, and reported the fact to the Emperor, who sent him reinforcements, and himself passed over the Nerbadda on his way to superintend the siege. On the 4th Ramazán the *Nauroz-i Sultáni* occurred, and His Majesty halted three days to celebrate the festival. * * The march of the Imperial force was then resumed.

Letters now arrived from *Nawáb 'Allámi* Shaikh Abú-l Fazl, who was coming from the Dakhin with the elephants and valuable effects of the late Prince, and who announced his arrival at Burhánpúr. He had received orders to join Shaikh Faríd, and to concert measures with him for the punishment of the recusant Prince. On the 4th Farwardín the army marched, and encamped at two *kos* distance from the fort of Ásír, because on that side there was no ground nearer the fort which was fit for a camp. Báz Bahádur Uzbek and Karábeg were sent forward immediately to select positions for the trenches and for the encampment of the besiegers.

On their return, they reported that they had never seen in any country a fort like this; for however long an army might press the siege, nothing but the extraordinary good fortune of the Emperor could effect its capture. Old soldiers, and men who had travelled into distant lands,—men who had seen the fortresses of Írán and Túrán, of Rúm, Europe, and of the whole habitable world, had never beheld the equal of this. It is situated on a high and strong hill, and three smaller hills, each having a fort, stand around it, like a halo round the moon. The ways of entrance and exit were difficult to discover.[1] Near it there was no other hill commanding it, and no way of approach. All around was level ground, and there were no trees or jungle to serve as cover. All the time the country had been held by the dynasty, each prince, as he succeeded, did his best to keep the place in repair, to add to its strength, or to increase its stores. It was impossible to conceive a stronger fortress, or one more amply supplied with artillery, warlike stores, and provisions. There were 500 *mans* of opium, *Akbar-sháhí* weight, in its stores. Were the fortress placed upon level ground, its reduction would be difficult; but such a hill, such a well-secured fortress, and such artillery, were not to be found in any one place on the face of the earth.

After the capture of the fortress accounts were taken of the munitions. Of pieces of artillery (*zarb-zan*), small and great, there were more than 1300, besides some which were disused. The balls varied in weight from nearly two *mans* down to a *sir* or a half *sir*. There were great numbers of mortars (*hukka-dán*), and also many *manjaniks*, each of which threw stones of 1000 or 2000 *mans*. On every bastion there were large iron cauldrons, in each of which twenty or thirty *mans* of oil could be boiled and poured down upon the assailants in case of assault. No account was taken of the muskets. Of provisions of all sorts, wines, medicines, aromatic roots, and of everything required for the use of man, there was vast abundance. When, after a protracted siege of eleven months, the place fell into the hands of the Imperial army, the quantities of

[1] Abú-l Fazl also gives a description of the fortress, and descants upon its great strength.

grain, oil, etc., which remained, after some thousands of men had been fed (during the siege), seemed as if the stores had never been touched. The stores of ammunition were such, that thousands of *mans* were left, although the quantity consumed had been enormous. For throughout the siege a constant firing was kept up night and day, with object and without object; so that in the dark nights of the rainy season no man dared to raise his head, and a demon even would not move about. There were large chambers full of powder. There were no springs of water in the fortress; but there were two or three immense reservoirs, in which the (rain) water was collected and stored from year to year, and amply sufficed for the requirements of the garrison. In the dwelling of each officer of importance there was a separate reservoir, containing a sufficient supply of pure water for his household. Nor had all this preparation been made for the occasion; it had been kept up from the foundation of the fortress. The rulers of the country had incessantly cared for the strengthening and provisioning of the fort, more especially in respect of artillery. The revenues of several *parganas* were specially and separately assigned to keep up the supply of artillery, so that the officers of the department had independent sources for maintaining its efficiency. The population in the fortress was like that of a city, for it was full of men of every kind. After the surrender, the inhabitants came out, and there was a continuous throng night and day for a week.

The houses of the chiefs were fine lofty buildings, and there were open spaces, gardens and fountains. In the walls of the fort, which were of great thickness, chambers and rooms were constructed for the officers of the artillery, where, during all seasons, they could live in comfort, and keep up a fire of cannon and musketry. The fortress has one gate, and outside this gate there is another fort called Kamargarh, the walls of which are joined on both sides to the great fort. This was looked upon as an outwork, and was held by inferior ranks of men, such as musketeers and archers. Below this fort, but still on an elevated spot, is another fort called Málgarh,[1] which also is very strong. In comparison with the fortress, it seems at the bottom of the earth; but compared with the surface of the ground, it looks half-way up to the sky. This being the most advanced of the works, great care had been taken to strengthen it with guns and other implements. Below this was an inhabited place called Takhati, as large as a city. In short, the fortress is one of the wonders of the world, and it is impossible to convey an idea of it to any one who has not seen it.

Shaikh Faríd, after collecting all available information about the fortress, wrote a description to the Emperor, and devoted himself to devising a plan for its capture. As the actual strength of the place was not fully known to the Emperor, envious men represented its reduction as being an easy matter, and thus vexed him. * * A letter at length arrived from the camp, announcing the Emperor's intention to come and examine into matters with his own eyes. About the same time also Shaikh Abú-l Fazl arrived from Burhánpúr, and encamped three or four *kos* from Ásír, as he was hastening to join the Emperor. He sent to inform Shaikh Faríd of his presence, and the Shaikh set off to see him. He had gone but a little way, when he remembered that Bahádur had promised to see him next day; so he stopped and returned to camp. Next day Bahádur came down from the fort to meet the Shaikh, and his spies busied themselves in observing all they could. It so happened that on that day a letter was coming from the Emperor, and the Shaikh mounted to go and meet it. But just as he was starting, his spies brought him word that the cavalcade was approaching. Although Shaikh Faríd had with him a large force of horse and foot, musketeers, rocket-men, and elephants, the matter seemed to him important, and he was apprehensive that there was some design against him. So he halted where he was, and sent a messenger to

[1] Abú-l Fazl says that information was obtained from one of the garrison of a secret way into this outwork, and that it was taken on a dark rainy night by a force under his command—an achievement which got him a great name.—*Akbar-náma*, vol. iii. p. 837; see Blochmann's *Áín-i Akbarí*, vol. i. p. xxiii.

Shaikh Abú-l Fazl, to say that he should not come to see him that day, as circumstances prevented him. * * Shaikh Faríd sent messengers to re-assure Bahádur, and he came with a large escort to the Shaikh's tent, and had an interview with him. Every argument was used to induce him to make his submission to the Emperor, and as he had no answer to give, he merely shook his head. At length he returned to his old excuse of being afraid, and rejecting all advice, he returned to the fortress. Some men have maintained that the Shaikh ought to have made him prisoner at this meeting; but resort to subterfuge and want of faith and truth never prove successful. Besides this, Bahádur had with him a force sufficient to resist the weak army of the Shaikh. Next day the Shaikh went to visit Shaikh Abú-l Fazl at his camp, three or four *kos* from the fortress, and the meeting with Bahádur was discussed, and a report sent off to the Emperor.

All expectation of Bahádur's submission being now given up, Abú-l Fazl, who had waited to see the result of the interview, proceeded to join the Emperor. Having first directed his attention to the occupation of the country, the closing of the roads, the way into and out of the fortress, the forming of the trenches, and other matters connected with the siege, Shaikh Faríd sent a detachment to Burhánpúr, to arrest the officers of Bahádur, and to occupy the city. But on arriving there, it was found that the governor had already made his submission to the Emperor. Some experienced officers thought it desirable that a force should be stationed there, * * and Shaikh Faríd finally decided that 1000 horse should be stationed between Burhánpúr and Asír. This force took up a position about two *kos* from the fortress, and cut off all communication between it and the city. Next day Shaikh Abú-l Barakát, brother of Shaikh Abú-l Fazl, joined the besieging force with the elephants and artillery which had been sent under his command. The army now removed to a more favourable position, and it was resolved to form trenches in every suitable place near the fort, and to close the roads and entrances. Another letter was received from Bahádur Khán, * * to which Shaikh Faríd replied. * * But Bahádur Khán trusted in the strength of his fort, and thought that its height and strength were such that no mortal force could take it.

One day when the commander rode towards the fort to examine it, a large gun was fired at him. It is related that some of the battlements of the tower on which it was placed fell down, and the gun itself also fell. This was received as a good omen by the Imperial army. Mír Sadr-i Jahán, who had returned to the Emperor, now came back, charged with an Imperial message. Next day Miyán Saiyid went round and looked after many things in the construction of the trenches, so that they might afford protection to the men, and enable them to stay there day and night. The Emperor's mind was intent upon this undertaking. Letters constantly arrived from him with instructions and urgent directions. Every day some one of his officers came to inspect and report upon the business of the siege. * *

Having received orders to wait upon the Emperor, Shaikh Faríd proceeded on the 18th to the royal camp at Búrgánw, seven or eight *kos* from Ásír. He was received very kindly, and he related all the details of the siege. He remained there the next day, and on the following day the Imperial camp moved towards Ásír. On the 21st Farwardín, or 25th Ramazán, it reached the city of Burhánpúr, and the Emperor took up his abode in the palace of the old rulers. Intent upon the siege, he then marched on, attended by numerous *amirs*, and arrived under the fort on the 3rd Shawwál. Shaikh Faríd then received orders to attend to his own duties as *Bakhshi*, and wait upon His Majesty, and to appoint the other *amirs* to the direction of the trenches, so that he might be ready, upon emergency, to lead a force in any direction.

The trenches were then allotted to the different *amirs*. The first to Khán-i 'Azam, * * another to Nawáb Ásaf Khán, another to Mirzá Jání Beg of Tatta * *. A fourth trench he placed in charge of his brethren and adherents, and having well examined it, he gave it into their charge, while he himself proceeded with a chosen force to attend upon the Emperor. It was impossible to dig mines or construct *sábáts;* so the men in each trench endeavoured to bring the investment as close as possible. At the end of the month, 'Azam Khán and Ásaf Khán reported that the garrison kept up a fire from different kinds of guns all night and day, with object and without object, necessary and unnecessary; and that the besiegers endured it with great bravery.

In the early days of Zí-l ka'da, Bahádur sent out of the fortress sixty-four elephants, along with his mother and son, to the Emperor, and begged forgiveness of his offences. The Emperor replied, that if he desired pardon, he must come out at once to make submission, and trust to the Emperor's mercy. * * On the 16th Zí-l hijja a sortie was made, in which many of the garrison lost their lives in a desperate struggle. When they were driven back, a little hill called Koriya fell into the hands of the besiegers. This eminence is so close to the fortress as to have command over it. The besiegers then saw that by occupying this commanding position, and by getting possession of another which was strongly fortified, they might overawe the garrison. The former masters of the place had seen the importance of this position, and had scarped the rock so that no one could climb up. * * * After hard fighting, this position was carried. * * *

On the 21st Safar news arrived of the capture of Ahmadnagar on the 18th. The fortress had long been defended by Chánd Báí, the sister of Nizámu-l Mulk, and when formerly besieged, dissensions among the Imperial *amírs* averted its capture. Prince Dániyál, assisted by some of the great *amírs*, had now taken it by assault. The siege had now been carried on for nearly six months, and a constant fire had been kept up without effect. Khán-knánán thought that mining must be resorted to, and the other *amírs* coinciding with him, a mine was formed. It was charged with 180 *mans* of gunpowder, and was exploded on the

20th Shahryúr, in the 45th year of the reign. A bastion was blown up with seventy or eighty *gaz* of the wall. Khán-khánán, Rájá Jagannáth, and the other *amirs*, exerted themselves to incite their troops, and gave orders that the troops were to rush in and finish the work directly after the explosion. This order was duly executed; and a force under Yúsuf Khán scaled the wall, by means of a mound,[1] in another place. The assailants pressed on, and after a severe fight, in which 1000 of the besiegers fell, the fortress was captured. The grandson of Nizámu-l Mulk was taken prisoner, and carried to the Emperor. * *

A few days after, Bahádur sent Sádát Khán and Shaikh Pír Muhammad Husain, two of his chief men, to the Emperor, with ten elephants and an entreaty for forgiveness. Two days afterwards Shaikh Pír Muhammad was sent back into the fortress, and Sádát Khan was kept as the guest of Shaikh Faríd. The escort which had come out with him was ordered to return with Pír Muhammad; but the men, about a hundred in number, declared that they would not return into the fortress and become prisoners (*asir*) in Ásír. Permission to remain was given to those who could give some bail that they would not run away, otherwise they were to be put in confinement. In the end some found the required bail, and some went back into the fortress.

Among the causes which brought about the surrender of the fortress was the impurity of the atmosphere, which engendered two diseases.[2] One was paralysis of the lower extremities, from the waist downwards, which deprived the sufferer of the powers of motion; the other was weakness of sight. These maladies greatly distressed and discouraged the men of the garrison, so that men of all ranks and degrees were of one mind and voice in urging Bahádur to capitulate. At their instance he wrote to the Emperor offering to surrender. The siege thus ended.

[1] [*Khák-rezi*, see *suprà*, p. 100.]

[2] [Abú-l Fazl says that the pestilence arose from the penning-up of more than 100,000 animals in the fortress; and that 25,000 human beings died from it.]

When Bahádur came out,[1] the Emperor held a grand *darbár*, at which all the great men were present, and Bahádur was amazed at the splendour and state. Mukarrib Khán, and several other of Bahádur's nobles, were sent into the fortress, in advance of Shaikh Abú-l Fazl, to inform the garrison of the surrender, and to require the giving up of the keys. When they approached, Mukarrib Khán's father mounted the top of the fort, and reviled him for having thrown his master into bonds and surrendered the fort. Unable to endure his abuse, the son stabbed himself two or three times in the abdomen, and a few days afterwards he died. On the 17th Safar the royal forces were admitted, and the keys were given up. * * * Khán-khánán, who had come from Ahmadnagar, went into the fortress and placed the royal seal on the treasure and warlike stores, which were then placed in charge of responsible officers. Just at this time Mirzá Jání Beg of Tatta died.

On the 8th Sha'bán the Emperor bestowed great honours on Shaikh Abú-l Fazl, including a banner and kettle-drums; and a hundred *amírs* were placed under his orders to assist in the subjugation of the Dakhin. Khán-khánán was sent to Ahmadnagar, and the general conquest of the Dahhin was committed to him. The Emperor went in and inspected the fortress. All the treasures and effects of Bahádur Khán, which had been collected by his ancestors during two hundred years, were brought out, and the wives and women of Bahádur, two hundred in number, were presented. The Emperor stayed in the place three days, and then proceeded to Burhánpúr. * *

On the 28th Shawwál all the country of the Dakhin, Birár, Khándesh, Málwa, and Gujarát were placed under the rule of Prince Dániyál.]